Chinese Characters, Deciphered

Antoine Bossard

神奈川大学出版会

Chinese Characters, Deciphered

by

Antoine BOSSARD

Original English edition published by Kanagawa University Press.
3-27-1 Rokkakubashi, Kanagawa-ku, Yokohama-shi, Kanagawa, 221-8686 JAPAN

© Antoine BOSSARD 2018
All rights reserved. No part of this book may be reproduced or transmitted in any form or by any
electronic or mechanical means, including photocopying, recording, or by any information
storage retrieval system, without permission.

ISBN 978-4-906279-14-2 C3004

Printed in Japan

À François

Contents

List of Figures   **ix**

List of Tables   **xi**

Foreword   **xv**

Preface – 前書   **xvii**

1   Introduction   **1**

2   About Chinese Characters   **9**
     2.1   History 10
     2.2   Geographical repartition 13
     2.3   Writing systems 17
         2.3.1   Traditional Chinese 18

vi   *Contents*

	2.3.2	Simplified Chinese	19
	2.3.3	Japanese	20
	2.3.4	Korean	22
	2.3.5	Chữ nôm	23
2.4	Local Chinese characters	24
	2.4.1	Japanese's *kokuji*	24
	2.4.2	Korean's *gukja*	28
	2.4.3	Chữ nôm's local characters	29
	2.4.4	Locally simplified characters	32

3 Conventional Description   **39**

3.1	Strokes	39
3.2	The six writings	44
3.3	Radicals	48
3.4	Pronunciation	51
3.5	Terminology	58

4 Character Relations   **65**

4.1	Notations and definitions	66
4.2	Morphological relations	68
	4.2.1	Ancestor-child relations	68
	4.2.2	Deriving layers and learning paths . . .	70
4.3	Semantic relations	73
4.4	Morpho-semantic relations	83
4.5	Phonetic relations	87
	4.5.1	Chinese and Korean	88

Contents vii

	4.5.2	Annamese	90
	4.5.3	Japanese	91
4.6		Particular phonetic relations: *dōkun-iji*	94

5 Character Algebra: Going Beyond Relations   **103**

5.1	The universal character set $\mathbb{U}$ 107
5.2	Composition operations 114
5.3	Character connectivity 126
5.4	Stroke order and connectivity 129
5.5	Automatic processing 132
5.6	From a statistical point of view 133
	5.6.1 Regular-use characters in Japanese . . . 135
	5.6.2 Teaching material for foreign students . 135

6 Ontological Discussion   **145**

6.1	Information model 146
6.2	Object instance examples 150

7 Applications   **157**

7.1	Universal character encoding 157
7.2	Character distance 162
	7.2.1 Morpho-semantic distance 162
	7.2.2 Mathematical distance 170
7.3	Character chains 176

viii   *Contents*

8 A Step Further   **181**
   8.1 Hinting at the semantics of the 亻+ operation . 182
       8.1.1 Analytic approach 185
       8.1.2 Census, analysis, and semantics 187
       8.1.3 A specificity of the *ninben* radical . . . 198
       8.1.4 Other (refuted) hypotheses 203
       8.1.5 To summarize 207
   8.2 Simplification reforms 208
   8.3 The case of Chữ nôm 213

9 Toward Practice   **219**

A Topmost Decomposition Operations   **227**

Acknowledgments   **233**

Index   **235**

List of Figures

2.1	Oracle bone, bronze, seal, and regular scripts. .	10
2.2	A timeline of the mentioned Chinese dynasties.	11
2.3	Geographical repartition of Chinese characters.	15
2.4	The Tangut script.	17
2.5	Photographs of locally simplified characters. . .	34
3.1	Painting directions for basic character strokes. .	41
4.1	The child and ancestor morphological relations.	70
4.2	From relations to layers and learning paths. . .	72
4.3	Semantic relations between characters.	82
4.4	The radical relation.	86
4.5	Phonetic relations between different dialects. .	89
4.6	Phonetic relations in Annamese.	92
4.7	The *on* phonetic relations in Japanese.	93

List of Figures

4.8	The *dōkun* relation.	97
4.9	Graphs from the *dōkun* and semantic relations.	99
5.1	Topmost operations: regular-use characters.	136
5.2	Topmost operations: first taught characters.	137
6.1	A Chinese character information model.	147
8.1	The two guardian gods of the Tenrinji temple.	193
8.2	Types of the characters of *ninben* radical.	200
8.3	Types of the characters of *gyōninben* radical.	203
8.4	Topmost operations: local Chữ nôm characters.	214
8.5	Assimilation of local Chữ nôm characters.	217

List of Tables

2.1	Variations between Taiwan and Hong-Kong. . .	18
2.2	Modern simplified Chinese characters.	19
2.3	China and Singapore simplification differences.	20
2.4	Character simplifications in 20th century Japan.	21
2.5	Japanese *kana* and Chinese characters.	22
2.6	*Kokuji* characters and their readings.	26
2.7	Korean's *gukja* local characters.	30
2.8	Chữ nôm local characters.	32
2.9	Locally simplified characters in Japanese. . . .	35
2.10	Locally simplified characters in Korean.	35
3.1	The eight basic character strokes.	40
3.2	The 36 character strokes as per Unicode (1). . .	42
3.3	The 36 character strokes as per Unicode (2). . .	43

xii   *List of Tables*

3.4	The pictogram character class.	46
3.5	Radicals holding the semantic information.	50
3.6	The conventional 214 radicals.	52
3.7	The three main *on* readings of Japanese.	56
4.1	New and old forms: Chinese and Japanese.	75
4.2	Japanese vulgar forms.	76
4.3	Tang dynasty Chinese vulgar forms.	77
4.4	Old and original form differences.	77
4.5	Ancient and original form differences.	78
4.6	Erroneous forms.	79
4.7	Alternative forms.	79
4.8	Character cosmetic changes.	81
5.1	The support set $\tilde{\mathbb{J}}$.	111
5.2	The composition operations in $\mathbb{U}$.	116
5.3	The first characters taught (1).	138
5.4	The first characters taught (2).	139
7.1	Distances with the δ metric.	166
7.2	Distances with the δ' and δ'' metrics.	169
7.3	Distances with the d metric.	175
8.1	Classification of the *ninben* characters.	199
8.2	Classification of the *gyōninben* characters.	202
8.3	Pronunciations of the selected characters.	206
8.4	New patterns induced by simplification.	209

List of Tables xiii

A.1 Regular-use characters: topmost operations (1). 228
A.2 Regular-use characters: topmost operations (2). 229
A.3 Regular-use characters: topmost operations (3). 230
A.4 Regular-use characters: topmost operations (4). 231
A.5 Regular-use characters: topmost operations (5). 232

xiv   *List of Tables*

Foreword

This book, "Chinese Characters, Deciphered," gives a scientific analysis for China-originating characters and their variants. These characters are striking for people who do not use them, though it would be incredibly difficult for them to learn and master the characters. The author, Dr. Antoine BOSSARD, was one such person when he participated in my laboratory as a Ph.D. candidate in computer science. However, he is now a very fluent Japanese language speaker and good at Japanese *kanji* writing. This book hints at the secret of why he has cultivated this ability so rapidly.

After the introduction of Chapter 1, the author gives contextual information about the characters in Chapter 2 and explains the basis of the characters in Chapter 3. Chapters 4 and

xvi   *Foreword*

5 form the essence of the book. Chapter 4 reveals the relationship among the forms, meanings, and sounds of the characters. We worked together on Chapter 5 to describe the relationship using mathematical algebra. In the remaining chapters, the author presents application examples based on the relationship proposed in Chapters 4 and 5.

Some readers may have a staid image for the word "scientific," but I hope that they will be stimulated by this book and sustain their interest in China-originating characters.

Professor Keiichi KANEKO, Ph.D.
Tokyo University of Agriculture and Technology

Preface – 前書

Started as a hobby, I have been exploring the fascinating world of Chinese characters for the past 15 years. A few years after my first real encounter with these intriguing symbols, I began my graduate studies in the field of information science and subsequently my research activities in graph theory. By graduation, I had already acquired 10 years of experience with Chinese characters. This is when I started considering these characters from a logical and computational point of view, thinking about a possible connection between Chinese characters and graph theory. Of course, as any other learner of these characters, I had relied more or less unconsciously on the relations, such as inclusion, that may exist between Chinese characters. Yet, it appeared that formally defining characters as graph vertices, linking them with edges of possibly different types, was not only possible and meaningful but also enabled diverse and important applications

xviii   *Preface – 前書*

such as providing significant supporting information for character memorization. These observations and research ideas led to the initiation of this book.

Formally defining the relations between Chinese characters was the first step and the core of this research. To this end, it was critical to analyze the various properties of the writing system as a whole for the considered script, for instance, Japanese. The next objective was to further enhance the logical structure that had been defined for Chinese characters. Concretely, this task consisted in covering the Chinese characters used across the multiple languages and scripts, then deriving character sets and composition operations. A character algebra was consequently induced, further extending the application range of our approach with, for instance, the introduction of the notion of distance between any two Chinese characters and that of character chains.

As a result, the logical and computational approach to Chinese characters proposed in this book differs significantly from conventional learning methodologies. By summarizing several years of research in the field, this book provides essential and insightful information not only for people seeking to efficiently prepare their future character memorization effort, but also for anyone willing to deeply and logically understand these captivating characters.

Preface – 前書　　xix

　私は、15年前に趣味として漢字の学習を始めました。数年後、大学院に入学し、数理情報科学のグラフ理論に関する研究をしました。大学院修了時には、約10年間、漢字を勉強した経験があり、このとき初めてグラフ理論と漢字との関係について考えました。それまでの数年間、漢字を覚え易くするため、無意識にこのような関係を利用していましたが、グラフの頂点を漢字とすることで、グラフの辺によって、漢字間の関係を定義することができ、漢字の学習を支援する貴重な情報となることを再認識しました。このことが、本書の源となっています。

　このアプローチでは、漢字間の関係を定義することが第一歩です。そのために、漢字だけでなく、文字体系全体の特徴を深く考える必要がありました。次に、日本の漢字だけではなく、中・日・韓・台・港・越など、様々な文化の漢字を包括する大きな漢字の集合に対する論理的な構成を考え始めました。これは漢字の「代数」となり、文字の連鎖や文字間の距離といった応用につながりました。

　本書で示す新しい科学的・論理的な漢字学習の方法は、一般の教材とは大きく異なり、学習者に対して大切な支援となることを信じて、数年間の研究成果を本書にまとめました。漢字の勉強を始めたい人に限らず、漢字を覚える前段階で、漢字の理解を深めるために本書を読んでいただけると幸いです。

xx   *Preface* – 前書

CHAPTER 1

Introduction

Numerous writing systems, with many interconnections, are in use across countries and ethnic groups, and even more if considering extinct scripts (refer, for example, to the works by Coulmas and Sampson as detailed at the end of this chapter). Chinese characters can be reasonably considered as the cement of Asian cultures. They are effectively found in many countries, languages, dialects, and scripts. Different countries may employ variants of the original, ancient characters. As examples, such characters are currently in use in mainland China with both the simplified and traditional scripts, Taiwan, Hong-Kong (each

2   *Introduction*

script having its own specificities, even if "Chinese"), Japan (the *kanji* script), Korea (the *hanja* script) to a lesser extent, and Annam (ancient Vietnam) with the Chữ nôm script. The actual number of Chinese characters remains unknown.

The objective of this book is to present Chinese characters: the motivation here is for the reader to gain a precise understanding of what Chinese characters are. This work should thus be seen as the first step before attempting to actually learn, memorize, and be proficient with Chinese characters. The author is convinced that such a preliminary step is the key to subsequent efficient learning of these characters. In other words, this book has not been written to memorize Chinese characters but to understand their nature in order to then facilitate their learning (memorization).

First and foremost, it should be clear that there is absolutely no prerequisite with respect to Chinese characters or the corresponding languages and cultures. On the contrary, this book is highly recommended for readers willing to start discovering the fascinating world of Chinese characters. Furthermore, it does not matter at which language, dialect, culture the reader is aiming: the characters are introduced here from a multicultural point of view. Thus, it is a good starting point for people interested in either Chinese, Taiwanese (Hokkien), Hong-Kongese (Cantonese), Japanese, and so on. In addition, this book will also be of high interest for readers interested in the study of writing systems and symbols in general, conducting rigorous anal-

Introduction 3

yses, such as relational analyses, with respect to the symbols used when dealing with Chinese characters. For instance, it is very likely that the runologist will find insightful information regarding ideograms, a type of symbol that would have been encountered occasionally with runes.

Books aimed at memorizing Chinese characters are widely available; selected works are presented in the closing chapter of this book (see Chapter 9). As explained previously, our objective is different. The approach followed here is that rather than conventionally giving a list of characters to which classic learning methods often have to resort, the rules and principles that structure Chinese characters are presented so as to efficiently prepare the memorization task. The three terms *rule*, *principle*, and *structure* are definitely key words here. This is a *scientific approach*, and even more precisely in some chapters, a *computational approach* to Chinese characters: each character is considered an object with properties, and various relations are defined between these objects. Such an ontological discussion is an important part of this book.

Let us next detail the rationale behind our approach. To start, the link is made with philosophy, which is relevant since, as explained previously, an ontological discussion will be conducted. Philosophy is not something one learns. Instead, philosophy is practiced, that is to philosophize. Because it is very close to philosophy, it can be reasonably assumed that a similar assertion can be made for mathematics. That is, mathematics

4   *Introduction*

is not something one learns. Instead, mathematics is practiced to gain familiarity with its utilization. Interestingly, this fundamental aspect of philosophy and mathematics has, even partially, disappeared from many, if not most, other disciplines. The reasons that can be suggested for this include the fact that various constraints bound the learner, for example, natural constraints for the geologist, physical ones for the physicist, and communication ones for the linguist. Hence, one somehow "simply" learns geology, physics, language.

Throughout this research, the author has been convinced that following a scientific approach to Chinese characters is the way to recover the freedom of practice, as with philosophy, which was kept at bay by the aforementioned learning constraints. So, by adopting a scientific, logical viewpoint when considering Chinese characters, the learner frees himself from the speech shackles, such as grammar, which are a sort of establishment for this Chinese character subject. As shown by Coulmas, writing should not be treated simply as a product of language.

Thanks to such a logical approach, thus hooking back to philosophy and mathematics, one is free to not only learn Chinese characters in the conventional sense but also practice them, *for example* treating the characters as elements of a set that are in relation with each other – *for example* is purposely stressed to show that with this approach, the learner is completely free with respect to the way objects, here characters, are treated. This aspect usually stays unrevealed to the language learner, and it

Introduction   5

should be regarded as a different, very natural method to approach Chinese characters.

In addition, when dealing with the writing systems of natural languages, and in particular with the sets of the glyphs used by the writing systems, punctual relations between these elements can be commonly noticed. Yet, because concerning natural languages, such sets are the results of empirical gathering over time, and it is thus very unlikely that these sets are assembled according to a logical structure. Given the numerous applications, and not only pedagogical ones, it is extremely interesting and meaningful to aim at uncovering and formalizing the relations between glyphs to eventually obtain a logical structure which would subsequently enable, for instance, facilitated computer processing and memorization by learners.

As a result, this book borrows notably from the fields of oriental languages and studies, writing systems, symbolics in general, computational linguistics, and, last but not least, logic. When relevant, and as already done a few paragraphs earlier, succinct comparison will be made with the runic writing system, as these two scripts sometimes share interesting properties.

This work has two main parts. The first includes Chapters 2 to 3, presenting Chinese characters rather conventionally but importantly from a global (international) point of view. The second part includes Chapters 4 to 9, conducting a deeper analysis by approaching Chinese characters from a scientific, and sometimes computational, viewpoint.

6   *Introduction*

When appropriate, we will rely on mathematical and logical notations so as to approach Chinese characters in the clearest and least ambiguous way possible. Although important with respect to the soundness of our method, these notations are not essential to understand this book: the reader may skip them with minimal inconvenience.

Bibliographical notes will be given at the end of each chapter. Because older manuscripts as mentioned in this book are not always accessible, more modern and thus more accessible materials will also be given in the bibliographical notes, mentioning, for instance, online resources in digital libraries and others. The reader should note that it is not often that English translations are available for the cited references. So, for the sake of clarity, the author will propose English translations for the reference titles when needed. It should be acknowledged that these are not official translations and are in no way endorsed by the respective authors.

Finally, each section of the chapters will include an illustration of a Chinese character that is related in some way to the content of the section, that is, a form of book illumination.

Bibliographical notes

1. Various major writing systems of our world, including Chinese characters, are reviewed by Florian Coulmas in

Bibliographical notes   7

his book "The writing systems of the world" (Oxford, England: Basil Blackwell, 1989). The author notably emphasizes the impact of writing on language whereas it is natural to think in the other way, precisely that writing derives from language.

2. A similar work was conducted by Geoffrey Sampson in his book "Writing systems" (Sheffield, England: Equinox Publishing, 1985, second edition in 2015), where the author also interestingly addresses the evolution of glyph shapes.

3. John DeFrancis in his book "Visible speech" (Honolulu, HI, USA: University of Hawaii Press, 1989) also discusses various writing systems including Chinese characters, with Chinese being the specialty of the author, and focusing particularly on phonetics.

4. As described in the book "Norwegian runes and runic inscriptions" by Terje Spurkland (Woodbridge, England: Boydell & Brewer, 2005), runes are sometimes used as ideograms, for example, the rune ᛗ used on its own in runic text for the meaning of "man," thus in a way linking runes to Chinese characters.

8   *Introduction*

CHAPTER 2

About Chinese Characters

In this chapter, a concise but global overview of Chinese characters is given, including their origin, the geographical repartition of their past and present usage, and the various writing systems relying on them.

10 *About Chinese Characters*

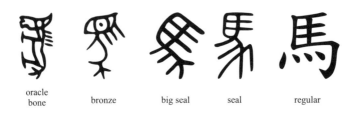

Figure 2.1: Illustrating the oracle bone, bronze, big seal, seal, and regular scripts with the character 馬 "horse."

2.1 History

Important milestones of the history of Chinese characters are presented in this section. Four main scripts are mentioned; they are illustrated in Figure 2.1. As usual with writing systems, a new version of the script does not suddenly replace the previous one. Hence, the scripts mentioned in this section should be seen as a blended evolution of Chinese characters, happening slowly over time until one script completely disappears. A similar evolution can be found, for example, with Scandinavian runes which slowly evolved from the elder fuþark alphabet toward short-twig and dotted runes. A timeline restricted to the Chinese dynasties mentioned in this book is given in Figure 2.2.

Chinese characters originate from what is now mainland China. Including some of the earliest traces of Chinese charac-

History 11

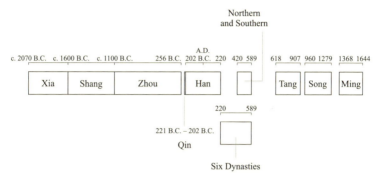

Figure 2.2: A timeline of the Chinese dynasties that are mentioned in this book.

ters, the oracle bone script was used for divination, with symbols (i.e., ancestors of modern Chinese characters) written on bones, such as ox shoulder blades or turtle shells (plastrons). The oracle bone script dates back to the late Shang dynasty, around 1200–1050 B.C. This script consists mostly of pictograms.

The bronze script is one major successor of the oracle bone script. It refers to characters written (molded) on bronzes such as cauldrons and bells, mostly for religious ornaments. The earliest evidence of the bronze script also dates back to the late Shang dynasty, but the most recent occurrences are from the Han dynasty (206 B.C.–220 A.D.), with obviously important style differences when comparing Shang and Han bronzes. As with the oracle bone script, the bronze script mostly involves pictograms. Unlike rune stones, the used materials for both the oracle bone and bronze scripts do not suffer too much from weathering. As such, numerous fragments are still accessible and readable today.

"history,"
"chronicle"

Next, the big seal script, followed by the (small) seal script, are representative of the Qin dynasty (221–206 B.C.); these are engraved scripts. Their usage became restricted to official seals from the Han dynasty as the Han dynasty saw the appearance of the (early) modern script, the clerical script, which later evolved to the regular (modern) script. On a side note, in addition to providing Qin dynasty seal examples, the book "The history of writing – China" by Chūkei Fushimi[1] remarkably shows illustrations of some of the earliest and rarest seals, dating back to the Yin (Shang) dynasty. According to Fushimi, the three Yin era seals represented therein – bronze seals unearthed in the Henan province – were very important finds, as they first proved the existence of seals during the Yin period.

As the materials used for inscriptions changed, that is from molded to engraved, and later came to be drawn and eventually written, the general shape of the characters changed, evolving from round shapes (oracle bone script), to strokes that tend to

---

[1] 書の歴史—中國篇— (in Japanese), Tokyo, Japan: Nigensha (二玄社), 1960.

Geographical repartition   13

be straight (regular script). As suggested by Sampson, this can be explained by the fact that molds were created with soft materials such as clay or wax, thus allowing for unrestricted line curving, that is, free hand drawing. Later scripts, engraved or painted, had to resort to straighter lines and smoother curves. This evolution from complex pictograms (oracle bone script) toward simpler shapes (regular script) is again to be compared with the evolution of runic writing, with simplifications such as short-twig, staveless, and dotted runes.

Finally, it is important to note that even if the Chinese characters as used in different languages and countries originate from a same source, language evolution has produced some semantic differences, and not necessarily minor ones, for a same character across the languages. For example, "pork" – in the common usage of the word, for instance, when referring to pork meat – is written in Japanese with the character 豚, whereas it is written with the character 猪 in modern Chinese, which means "boar" in Japanese.

2.2   Geographical repartition

A simplified overview of the geographical repartition of the writing systems based on Chinese characters is given in Figure 2.3. This map only emphasizes countries whose official languages include at least one which relies, possibly partly, on Chi-

14 *About Chinese Characters*

nese characters. Although they constitute a large population of individuals (50 million being a consensus), overseas Chinese communities are not represented on this map.

"land,"
"earth"

First and foremost, for historical reasons, mainland China is at the center of Chinese characters' usage. Yet, the Chinese characters used in mainland China nowadays differ from the ones used in earlier times. Mainland China now relies on simplified Chinese, a writing system that is based on simplified Chinese characters (see Section 2.3.2).

The Chinese characters used in Taiwan, Hong-Kong, and Macao did not undergo the simplification process as in mainland China. The writing systems of these regions are based on traditional Chinese characters (see Section 2.3.1). One should note that even if they share their writing system (with some minor differences though), the languages in use may differ. For example, Mandarin Chinese is the official language of Taiwan, whereas Cantonese is the official language of Hong-Kong and Macao.

In Japan, several different sets of characters are used: not only Chinese characters (referred to as *kanji*) but also characters specific to Japan, which are (almost) unrelated to Chinese characters. As China, Japan has simplified several Chinese characters for its usage, yet the simplifications made are distinct from those of China. The Japanese writing systems are further dis-

Geographical repartition 15

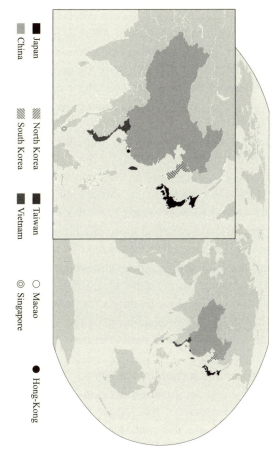

Figure 2.3: Simplified repartition of Chinese characters' usage.

16 *About Chinese Characters*

cussed in Section 2.3.3.

The usage of Chinese characters in Korea is nowadays very limited. Mostly, they are used for proper nouns such as person and place names. In addition, there are some specific cases with occurrences of Chinese characters, for example South Korea sometimes refers to North Korea using the 北 "north" Chinese character.

Mandarin Chinese is one of the four official languages of Singapore and also the one spoken by the most Singaporeans. As such, Chinese characters are an important part of Singapore's culture. Since 1969, traditional Chinese characters have been replaced by simplified ones. Since 1976, the simplified characters of Singapore have matched those of China.

On the verge of extinction, the usage of Chinese characters in Vietnam, the Chữ nôm script, is almost non-existent nowadays, being restricted to ceremonial and decorative purposes. This script is now understood by only a few scholars worldwide. Chinese characters have been replaced by the Latin alphabet extended with several diacritics partly because of influence from French colonial rule.

To conclude this section on the geographical repartition of Chinese characters, we mention a related script: the Tangut script (a.k.a. *xixia* script). The Tangut language and its script were used in parts of Tibet and Burma at least from the 11th century until the 16th century. Three sample Tangut characters are given in Figure 2.4 (from left to right: "dustpan," "wizard," and "obvious") for an informal comparison with Chinese characters.

"Tangut Yinchuan" font – copyright Jing Yongshi

Figure 2.4: The Tangut script: early relatives of Chinese characters.

2.3 Writing systems

"open," as used in Singapore

Here, we describe in more detail and with multiple examples the various writing systems that rely on Chinese characters. The purpose of this section is not to formally and exhaustively describe the writing systems mentioned but rather to give a short introduction which will provide contextual information for our discussion of Chinese characters throughout this book.

18   *About Chinese Characters*

2.3.1   Traditional Chinese

Traditional Chinese refers to the usage of Chinese characters as they are listed in the *Kāngxī* dictionary (18th century). Even though evolution has been witnessed with respect to the shape of some characters, the characters of the *Kāngxī* dictionary have been considered stable since the Northern and Southern dynasties (420–589 A.D.). Traditional Chinese is in use in Taiwan, Hong-Kong, and Macao but with a few character differences. Examples of character variations (i.e., variants of a same character) are given in Table 2.1: the first row includes characters as used in Taiwan, and the second includes the corresponding character variants as used in Hong-Kong. Each such pair of characters in this table consists of two distinct variants of a same character. Effectively, and as detailed in Chapter 4, a single character may have several different writings possible – these writings are often related in some ways – for instance, the old form, vernacular form, and orthodox form of a single character.

Table 2.1: Several examples of character variations in traditional Chinese between Taiwan and Hong-Kong.

| Taiwan | 裡 | 峰 | 群 | 麵 | 線 | 村 |
| Hong-Kong | 裏 | 峯 | 羣 | 麪 | 綫 | 邨 |

Writing systems 19

2.3.2 Simplified Chinese

Simplified Chinese results from the successive simplification reforms undergone in China during the 20th century. Simplifications have been witnessed throughout the centuries. However, if we focus on the 20th century, simplification proposals starting in as early as 1909 (K. Lubi), this issue was addressed for the first time by the Chinese government in the 1930s, with the first set of 324 simplified characters issued officially in 1935. Examples of simplified characters and the corresponding traditional ones are given in Table 2.2.

Table 2.2: Examples of simplified characters as used in simplified Chinese nowadays.

Traditional	長	業	見	個	関
Simplified	长	业	见	个	关

As mentioned previously, between 1969 and 1976, Singapore used simplified Chinese characters but with a few differences compared to the simplified characters used in China. Examples of different versions of simplified characters for China and Singapore are given in Table 2.3, with the traditional character forms also given for reference.

20   *About Chinese Characters*

Table 2.3: Examples of different character simplifications between China and Singapore (1969–1976).

Traditional	開	來	發	惡	場
Simplified (China)	开	来	发	恶	场
Simplified (Singapore)	闬	耒	発	悪	坊

2.3.3 Japanese

As briefly mentioned, several writing systems are in use in Japan, including Chinese characters. First, the Chinese characters used in Japan nowadays differ from those used in earlier times, and this is again due to the simplification reforms adopted by the Japanese government (the simplification process started in 1946, with the table of simplified characters officially announced in 1949). Examples of character simplifications are given in Table 2.4; it is customary to speak of new and old forms. The simplifications adopted by Japan differ from those adopted by China. For example, the character 樂 "comfortable" has been simplified to 乐 in China and to 楽 in Japan.

Unlike the Chinese writing system which relies exclusively on Chinese characters, the Japanese writing system also relies on specific character sets, the *kana* characters. *Hiragana* and *katakana* are the two most common *kana* character sets. Comparable to the Latin alphabet, *kana* characters are phonetic

Writing systems 21

Table 2.4: Examples of character simplifications which took place in Japan in the 20th century.

Old form	亞	鹽	驛	圖	聲
New form	亜	塩	駅	図	声

letters with no meaning assigned. *Kana* characters are originally derived from Chinese characters as illustrated in Table 2.5 (pronunciation given with the International Phonetic Alphabet (IPA)). In modern Japanese, these characters are used for grammatical and pronunciation purposes. As such, they are sometimes referred to as the orthography of the language (as mentioned, for instance, by Tsuneari Fukuda[2]).

Unlike *kokuji* characters, which are also characters localized to a specific country (see Section 2.4), for instance Japan, *hiragana* and *katakana* are not considered Chinese characters as they only derive from them.

Finally, it should be noted that other writing systems were in use in Japan at some point in the past but almost absent from modern Japanese. Such character sets include, for example, *hentaigana* and *sōgana*, which are, as *hiragana* and *katakana*, derived from Chinese characters but not considered Chinese characters. Another interesting character set example is the Tai-

---

[2]"My Japanese language school" (私の國語教室, in Japanese), Tokyo, Japan: Shinchosha (新潮社), 1960.

22   *About Chinese Characters*

Table 2.5: Excerpt of *kana* characters illustrating their ancient relation to Chinese characters.

Transcription	[a]	[i]	[ɯ]	[e]	[o]
Origin	安	以	字	衣	於
Katakana	ア	イ	ウ	エ	オ
Hiragana	あ	い	う	え	お

wanese *kana*, based on *katakana* and used while Taiwan was under Japanese rule (1896–1945).

2.3.4   Korean

Both North and South Korea use the Hangul phonetic alphabet as their main writing system. Nevertheless, Hangul has coexisted with Chinese characters (referred to as *hanja* in Korean) for centuries. Yet, it should be noted that the usage of *hanja* nowadays has significantly decreased, the knowledge of Korean people with respect to Chinese characters declining. The surviving usages of Chinese characters in Korea are mainly for proper nouns, for instance, person names and place names, religious and decorative uses. Other uses include newspaper titles and emphasis. For instance, North Korea is often referred to as 北 "north." This declining usage can be seen as the main reason for that no simplification reform was conducted in the Korean

Writing systems   23

peninsula, in contrast to China and Japan. As such, the Chinese characters used in Korea are of traditional form, comparable to those used in traditional Chinese (but with some differences though). It is worth noting that some Chinese characters are local to Korea, comparable to Japan's *kokuji*. These are the *gukja* characters (see Section 2.4).

2.3.5   Chữ nôm

Until the beginning of the 20th century, Vietnam, also referred to as Annam depending on the period, relied on Chữ nôm, a writing system based on Chinese characters. Partly because of French colonial influence, Chữ nôm was replaced since the 1920s by the Latin alphabet extended by several diacritics. Regarding Chữ nôm, to accommodate Vietnamese pronunciation, several Chinese characters were created from existing ones, thus producing characters local to Vietnam (see Section 2.4). Hence, as, for example, Japanese and Korean, Chữ nôm comprises Chinese characters and local (Chinese) characters, but Chữ nôm relies significantly more on local Chinese characters than the Japanese and Korean scripts. Notably, one of the most well-known Vietnamese works of literature, the poem *The Tale of Kiều* (傳翹 in Chữ nôm) is written using the Chữ nôm script. Nowadays, Chữ nôm is only understood by a few scholars. This writing system is therefore in great danger of extinction.

24   *About Chinese Characters*

2.4   Local Chinese characters

In this section, we give an overview of Chinese characters locally created, i.e., characters specific to a country or region. These characters, being based on Chinese characters (though absent from Chinese), are still considered as Chinese characters for clarity. We focus on the cases of Japan, Korea, and Vietnam.

2.4.1   Japanese's *kokuji*

"country,"
"kingdom"

Early Japanese and Chinese languages existed independently (*yamatokotoba* is a common appellation when referring to early spoken Japanese). Chinese characters were then imported by Japan as part of the Japanese writing system, assigning to a Japanese word, when possible, the Chinese character in use in China at that time whose meaning corresponded to that of the original Japanese word. For example, the Japanese word *mizu* "water" is assigned to the Chinese character 水 whose meaning is identical. Yet, several issues arose: what about original Japanese words that did not have a corresponding term in Chinese? A conventional example is that of natural species (e.g., botanical species) found in the Japanese isles but not in China. For such cases, Japan had to introduce new characters: the *kokuji* characters (a.k.a. *wasei kanji*). Hence, while Chinese characters (*kanji*, thus non-*kokuji*) in use

Local Chinese characters   25

in Japan have both Chinese and Japanese readings (*on* and *kun*, respectively; character readings are detailed in the next section), most Japan-original *kokuji* characters only have Japanese pronunciations (i.e., *kun*). There are a few exceptions though, with a few *kokuji* characters having both or only *on* readings (see Table 2.6). Besides natural species and phenomenons, the Edo period work *Kokujikō* (國字考) by Naokata Ban, as referred to by the Encyclopedia Nipponica,[3] also lists human features (e.g., anatomy), living (e.g., food, clothing), materials (including tools), and language-related *kokuji* characters.

There are numerous *kokuji* characters, even though it is not clear for several characters whether they are *kokuji* or *kanji* characters (that is, whether they first appeared in Japan or China). Hence, there are several counts in the literature: 81 are given in the 1760 work *Dōbun tsūkō* (同文通考) by Hakuseki Harai, 126 in the 18th–19th century work *Kokujikō* (國字考) by Naokata Ban, and 641 (without variants) are listed in the more modern "The *kanji* characters made by Japanese people – diverse issues of local characters" by Etsuko Obata Reiman.[4] Yet, a large part of these *kokuji* characters remain rarely used. For instance, natural species are sadly often written phonetically with *katakana* characters rather than with the corresponding Chinese charac-

---

[3] 日本大百科全書 (in Japanese), Tokyo, Japan: Shogakukan (小学館), 2001.

[4] 日本人の作った漢字―国字の諸問題 (in Japanese), Tokyo, Japan: Nan'Un-Do (南雲堂), 1990.

26 *About Chinese Characters*

Table 2.6: Examples of *kokuji* characters and their readings, *on* readings being rare for *kokuji* characters.

kokuji	*on* reading	*kun* reading	Translation
峠	-	*tōge*	mountain pass
凪	-	*nagi*	calm
凩	-	*kogarashi*	cold wind
雫	-	*shizuku*	drop of water
鱇	*kō*	-	鮟鱇: anglerfish
腺	*sen*	-	gland
鋲	*byō*	-	drawing pin
働	*dō*	*hataraki*	work

ters (for a simplified reading, in the sense of pronunciation, but arguably at the cost of readability, in the sense of understanding). A common approach when "designing" new characters for words specific to Japan was to semantically combine two existing Chinese characters (i.e., compound ideographs, see Section 3.2). Several examples are given in the following paragraph.

The *kokuji* characters are found in Japanese as early as the Nara period (710–794 A.D.), with, for example, the *kokuji* character 蘰 "climbing plant" attested in the 7th–8th century *Manyōshū* (萬葉集) poem compilation (e.g., the poem no. 149

for the *kokuji* character 蘰). Moreover, it is worth noting that numerous *kokuji* characters were introduced during the Meiji period (1868–1912), the era that saw Japan transition from a feudal society to a modern one, inducing new relations to foreign cultures and techniques, with new words thus appearing to describe freshly imported concepts, such as, for example, 母音 "vowel" and 子音 "consonant." At that time, following this modernization trend, attempts at character merging were made, likely for convenience. For example, the rather infrequent *kokuji* characters 轏 "train" and 俥 "ricksha (man-pulled car)," which both merge the corresponding Chinese character writings, 電車 and 人車, respectively. In addition, based on the three Chinese characters 米, 立, and 瓦, which can be used besides their original meanings for the meter, liter, and gram units, respectively, several *kokuji* characters were created in Japanese to describe international scientific units such as 粁 "kilometer" (千 "thousand"), 竍 "decaliter" (十 "ten"), and 瓸 "hectogram" (百 "hundred").

Interestingly, several *kokuji* characters, that is first invented in Japan, were exported back to China and are currently in use there. Examples of such characters include 畑 "field" and 腺 "gland."

In closing this section, it is worth mentioning that several Chinese characters used in Japanese have meanings that differ from those of the original characters. This phenomenon is called the *kokkun* readings. This corresponds to the usage of Chinese characters that is local to Japanese and, hence, related to *kokuji*

28   *About Chinese Characters*

characters. However, since these characters are not new, i.e., reused as is but with a different meaning, they are not discussed in this section.

2.4.2   Korean's *gukja*

Korean also has its own local characters that are based on existing Chinese ones. Such characters local to Korean are called the *gukja* (國字) characters, that is the same word as in Japanese: *kokuji* is also written 國字 (国字 if using modern characters) in Japanese. There are very few *gukja* characters in comparison to Japanese *kokuji* characters and Annamese ones (refer to the next section). Comparable to the local characters of the other languages, the *gukja* characters are most of the time used to represent objects that are exclusive to Korea, including proper nouns, or to provide characters for words whose pronunciations do not match any existing Chinese character.

The *gukja* characters can be divided into the following two main categories:

Type 1

These are new characters that combine existing Chinese characters, usually two. Such character combinations are mostly phono-semantic compounds and semantic compounds (more details on character compounds are given in Chapter 3).

Type 2

These are new characters that add to an existing Chinese character a small, characteristic part, often derived from Hangul, e.g., ㄱ, ㅁ, and 乙 (i.e., ㄹ).

Examples are given in Table 2.7. Interestingly, both Korean and Japanese resorted to local characters to distinguish the different types of fields, carefully distinguishing rice fields from others. While Japanese relies on the local character 畑 to denote a field and on the Chinese character 田 to denote a paddy (rice) field, Korean does the opposite: the local character 畓 is used to denote a paddy (rice) field and the Chinese character 田 is used to denote a field.

In addition, comparable to Japanese's *kokkun*, *gukja* characters also include existing Chinese characters used for words whose meanings are unrelated to the original ones, thus being local character usages. For instance, the character 串 has the original meaning of "broach, skewer" but when used in Korean means "cape, promontory." Because they are not new characters, they are not discussed in this section.

2.4.3 Chữ nôm's local characters

In comparison with the local characters introduced in the Korean, and even Japanese languages, the number of local characters in Annamese is very large, comprising thousands of characters. They are split into the following three categories:

30   *About Chinese Characters*

Table 2.7: Examples of Korean's *gukja* local characters.

	gukja	Reading	Translation
Type 1	畓	*dap*	paddy field
	媤	*si*	[husband's] home
	欌	*jang*	wardrobe
	䭏	*pyeon*	rice cake
Type 2	乭	*dol*	(only phonetic purpose for proper nouns; no meaning)
	乤	*hal*	
	乶	*bol*	
	旕	*geok*	

Phono-semantic compounds

This is the main group of local Chữ nôm characters and of Chinese characters in general. For an Annamese word *w*, a Chữ nôm character of this sort combines two Chinese characters, one whose reading matches the pronunciation of *w*, and the other one whose meaning matches that of *w*. A typical example is the Annamese word *ba* "three" (among other meanings) written with the local Chữ nôm character 𠀧 *ba*, which combines the character 巴 for its Chinese reading *ba* and the character 三 for its meaning "three." Another example is the Annamese word *năm*

Local Chinese characters   31

"year" (among other meanings) written with the local Chữ nôm character 蚌 *năm*, which combines the character 南 for its Chinese reading *nán* and the character 年 for its meaning "year."

Semantic compounds

A Chữ nôm character of this sort again combines two Chinese characters, but this time, both for their respective meanings, and sometimes the respective meanings of the characters are close enough. Even though it is sometimes difficult to be assertive regarding classification, the local Chữ nôm characters 跢 *sánh* "compare" combining 並 and 多 (both "several"), 矓 *trõm* "cavernous [eyes]" combining 目 and 覽 (both "see"), and 丕 *trời* "heaven" combining 天 and 上 (both "above") can be regarded as semantic compounds.

Modified Chinese characters

Finally, some local Chữ nôm characters are modified versions of Chinese characters, often simplified versions. They are very few, and the most well-known are probably 仒 *ấy* "that," which derives from the Chinese character 衣, and 仒 *làm* (usually styled 乕 or 𠃤 in Annamese) "make," which is assumed to derive from 濫 *lạm*.

A few other examples of local Chữ nôm characters that are phono-semantic compounds are given in Table 2.8. Common to

32   *About Chinese Characters*

Table 2.8: Examples of Chữ nôm local characters that are phono-semantic compounds.

Chữ nôm	Reading	Translation	Semantic root
㑲	*nay*	now	今 "now"
嫩	*non*	mount	山 "mountain"
𩥁	*đuôi*	end	尾 "tail"
捴	*ngón*	finger	手 "hand"
壌	*vung*	lid	土 "soil"

the other languages, phono-semantic and semantic compounds are further detailed in Chapter 3.

2.4.4   Locally simplified characters

Even though the definitions may vary, for instance, by whether they include official simplified forms, locally simplified characters here are defined as characters that are not officially recognized as correct by the respective languages but instead unofficial "abbreviations." For example, even though the local Chữ nôm character 伙 *ấy* is effectively a locally simplified version of the Chinese character 衣, because 伙 is officially recognized as a proper, correct Chữ nôm character, it does not fall into this section.

Local Chinese characters   33

Such unofficial character "abbreviations" mostly concern Japanese and Korean since Chinese has already undergone significant official simplification reforms, while Annamese was presumably not in use for a long enough time, or with a large enough literate population, for the need to abbreviate characters to emerge. In fact, some locally simplified characters in Japanese correspond to official simplifications in Chinese. For instance, in Japanese the character 魚 is a local simplification of the character 魚, but at the same time, 鱼 is the official Chinese simplified form of 魚. In Japanese, such locally simplified characters are referred to as *ryakuji* (略字), and as *yakja* in Korean. The obvious aim of such characters is to facilitate writing. Because they are not considered as correct, they would not be found in documents. However, shop and road signs are a common usage of locally simplified characters.

A photograph is presented in Figure 2.5a, which shows a Japanese water meter access chamber on the ground reading 量水器 "water meter" but interestingly with the locally simplified character 㐂 for the character 器. Practical issues, such as shape embossing, are likely explanations for the use of such a locally simplified character. Another photograph is given in Figure 2.5b, which partially shows a Japanese parking sign that includes a local simplification of the character 駐 (the full sign says 駐車禁止 "no parking"). In this particular case, it is most likely that simplification of the character shape has been required given the width of the brush used to paint the sign. The

34   *About Chinese Characters*

(a)

(b)

Figure 2.5: Photographs showing locally simplified characters as used in Japan for a water meter (a) – 器 being simplified – and a parking sign (b) – 駐 being simplified.

width was probably too large to allow for the reproduction of all the character shape (stroke) details.

Additional examples in the case of Japanese are given in Table 2.9, with the three simplified characters 試, 材, and 広 being examples of simplifications by means of the phonetic (*katakana*) glyphs corresponding to the character *on* readings: ギ *gi*, キ *ki*, and マ *ma*, respectively. Examples in the case of Korean are given in Table 2.10. Such simplifications are some-

Table 2.9: Examples of locally simplified characters as found in Japanese (i.e., *ryakuji*). Regular and simplified characters are given.

Reg.	**Simpl.**	**Reg.**	**Simpl.**	**Reg.**	**Simpl.**
第	才	門	冂, 门	選	⿺辶⿱乂关
品	品	器	噐	議	⿰言乂
魚	鱼, 奥	職	⿰耳厶, 耺	機	⿰木戈, ⿰木キ
濾	沪	曜	⿰日玉, 旺	摩	⿸广マ

times reused further for characters that include such characters as sub-elements. For instance, in Japanese the simplification of the character 門 into 门 can also be witnessed with the character 間 *aida* "interval" being abbreviated 间.

Table 2.10: Examples of locally simplified characters as found in Korean (i.e., *yakja*).

Regular	**Simplified**	**Regular**	**Simplified**
無	⿱𠂉亐	麗	⿱丽比
驛	⿰馬月	廣	庇
權	权		

36   *About Chinese Characters*

Bibliographical notes

1. The origins of the Japanese *kana* writing system, including the ancient *hentaigana* script, are detailed in the book "A history of the Japanese language" by Bjarke Frellesvig (Cambridge, England: Cambridge University Press, 2010). As an illustration, numerous characters written with styles of the oracle bone, bronze, and two seal scripts are given in the very accessible compendia *Kōkotsu jiten* (甲骨字典, 2016), *Kinbun jiten* (金文字典, 2014), *Shōten jiten* (小篆字典, 2014) and *Inten jiten* (印篆字典, 2014), all by Tōten Watahiki (Tokyo, Japan: Nigensha (二玄社)).

2. The two-volume Taiwanese-Japanese dictionary 臺日大辭典 (originally edited and published by the Office of the Governor-General of Taiwan (臺灣總督府) in 1931–1932, and republished in 1993 (Taipei, Taiwan: Woolin (武陵出版社)) is a good illustration of the usage of Taiwanese *kana*. The original edition is available in the National Diet Library of Japan, including its online repository.

3. Relying on older materials, the French bishop Jean-Louis Taberd gathered the "Dictionarium Anamitico-Latinum," reference work with respect to the Chữ nôm script. This Annamese-Latin dictionary was first published in 1884

Bibliographical notes   37

in Bengal. A second publication has been available since 2004 from the National Studies Center and the Literature Publishing House, Saigon, Vietnam.

4. A Tangut-Chinese dictionary (夏漢字典) has been edited by Fan Wen Li (Beijing, China: China Social Sciences Press (中國社會科學出版社), 1997, corrected edition in 2008). This dictionary also includes English translations and transliterations.

5. Local characters as used in Japanese (i.e., *kokuji*) are discussed, for instance, in the book "Strange local characters" (奇妙な国字, in Japanese) by Tatsuo Nishii (Tokyo, Japan: Gentosha Renaissance (幻冬舎ルネッサンス), 2009), with, in particular, the two insightful *kokuji* examples 燵 (as in 火燵 "kotatsu (a heated covered low table)") and 纐 (as in 纐纈 "kōkechi (a tie-dye of the Nara period)") thoroughly analyzed.

6. A digitalized version of the 18th century (1760) seven-volume book "*Dōbun tsūkō*" (同文通考, in Japanese) by Hakuseki Harai, which lists 81 *kokuji* characters, is available online from the Waseda University library. Rare *kokuji* characters such as 桵 "colored leaves," 椻 "Japanese lime," and 朤 "moonlight" are included.

7. Finally, the very recent book "Local character dictio-

38   *About Chinese Characters*

nary" (「国字」字典, in Japanese) by Hiroyuki Sasahara
(Tokyo, Japan: Sekaibunka-sha (世界文化社), 2017)
dedicated to Japanese *kokuji* characters provides a comprehensive list of these particular characters, classify-
ing them into six main categories: land, animal, human,
life, living, and geographic. The book reviews numerous
kokuji characters, including infrequent forms such as 軕
"train."

CHAPTER 3

Conventional Description

In this chapter, Chinese characters and their properties are presented in a traditional way, thus laying the foundation for further analysis in subsequent chapters.

3.1 Strokes

Chinese characters consist of one or several strokes. Character strokes were originally painted with a calligraphic brush (paintbrush), which explains the way (i.e., direction of the brush)

40   Conventional Description

Table 3.1: The eight basic strokes as given by Coulmas used to draw Chinese characters. Both Chinese and Japanese readings are given for each stroke.

Stroke	Name	Reading (Chi. / Jap.)	Meaning
丶	点	diǎn / ten	dot
一	横	héng / yoko	horizontal
丨	竖	shù / tate	vertical
丿	撇	piě / hidari harai	left-falling
乀	捺	nà / migi harai	right-falling
乁	提	tí / hane	rising
亅乚𠃊乀	鈎	gōu / hane, kagi	hook
乛⏋	折	zhé / ore	turning

strokes are painted, or simply written with a pen in our modern era.

"stroke,"
"drawing"

Coulmas (see bibliographical notes) gives the eight basic strokes of Chinese characters. These are shown in Table 3.1. Each stroke has a name, which derives from the stroke shape or look. How strokes are drawn is illustrated in Figure 3.1 with several examples taken from the basic strokes of Table 3.1.

In addition to these eight basic strokes, several others are

Strokes 41

Figure 3.1: Examples of stroke painting directions for basic strokes. Chinese stroke names are given for reference.

often considered. For instance, the Unicode standard gives the 36 strokes (range 31C0–31EF of the Basic Multilingual Plane (BMP) plane) listed in Tables 3.2 and 3.3. For each stroke, one actual character that includes it is given as an example.

Finally, the strokes that make a character are drawn in a particular order, referred to as the writing order. The writing order of every character is not absolutely defined and may thus vary from one ethnic group to another. Yet, official guidelines regarding the writing order are often defined by governmental authorities such as the Japanese Ministry of Education. As mentioned by the Heibonsha World Encyclopedia,[1] the writing order of a character results from writing efficiency (e.g., paintbrush manipulation) and rationality as inferred during early ages. As such, the writing order is considered by some as an important aspect of character memorization (likely relying on kinesthetic

---
[1] 世界大百科事典, second edition, Tokyo, Japan: Heibonsha (平凡社), 1998.

42   *Conventional Description*

Table 3.2: The 36 strokes used to draw Chinese characters as per the Unicode standard – Part I (range 31C0–31D1).

Stroke	Name	Reading (Chinese)	Example
㇀	提	*tí*	准
㇁	彎鈎	*wān gōu*	狸
㇂	斜鈎	*xié gōu*	浅
㇃	扁斜鈎	*biǎn xié gōu*	心
㇄	竪彎	*shù wān*	忙
㇅	横折折	*héng zhé zhé*	凹
㇆	横折鈎	*héng zhé gōu*	司
㇇	横撇	*héng piě*	今
㇈	横折彎鈎	*héng zhé wān gōu*	風
㇉	竪折彎鈎	*shù zhé wān gōu*	弓
㇊	横折提	*héng zhé tí*	说
㇋	横折折撇	*héng zhé zhé piě*	庭
㇌	横折彎鈎	*héng piě wān gōu*	部
㇍	横折彎	*héng zhé wān*	設
㇎	横折折折	*héng zhé zhé zhé*	凸
㇏	捺	*nà*	人
㇐	横	*héng*	三
㇑	竪	*shù*	中

Strokes 43

Table 3.3: The 36 strokes used to draw Chinese characters as per the Unicode standard – Part II (range 31D2–31E3).

Stroke	Name	Reading (Chinese)	Example
㇒	撇	*piě*	父
㇓	竪撇	*shù piě*	机
㇔	點	*diǎn*	丼
㇕	橫折	*héng zhé*	口
㇖	橫鈎	*héng gōu*	子
㇗	竪折	*shù zhé*	山
㇙	竪彎折	*shù wān zhé*	淵
㇚	竪提	*shù tí*	以
㇛	竪鈎	*shù gōu*	水
㇜	撇点	*piě diǎn*	巡
㇝	撇折	*piě zhé*	公
㇞	提捺	*tí nà*	入
㇟	竪折折	*shù zhé zhé*	亞
㇠	竪彎鈎	*shù wān gōu*	礼
㇡	橫斜彎鈎	*héng xié wān gōu*	乞
㇢	橫折折折鈎	*héng zhé zhé zhé gōu*	乃
㇣	撇鈎	*piě gōu*	乄
○	圏	*quān*	㐀

44 Conventional Description

memory). In general, a character's strokes are drawn from top to bottom and from left to right. For example, the character 立 is written in the stroke order 丶, 一, ｜, ｜, 一, and the character 目 is written in the stroke order ｜, ㇕, 一, 一, 一. To illustrate the writing order differences that can arise between different scripts, we mention the character 必, notorious for its confusing stroke order, which is written in the order 丶 (top), ノ, ㇌, 丶 (left), 丶 (right) in Japanese, in the order 丶 (left), ㇌, 丶 (top), ノ, 丶 (right) in Chinese, and in the order 丶 (left), ㇌, 丶 (top), 丶 (right), ノ in Taiwanese. This can be confusing indeed. Character writing order will be further discussed in Section 5.4.

3.2 The six writings

"land," but also "six"

Chinese characters are conventionally classified according to two methods. The first classification method is by using character radicals, which is the subject of the next section (Section 3.3). The second method is that of the 六書 "six writings," or *liùshū* in Chinese and *rikusho* in Japanese. The six writings classification is usually considered older than the radical classification. Its usage is confirmed in the 2nd century *Shuōwén jiězì* dictionary, and it might be even older, even though there may be some debate. In any case, it is

The six writings 45

much older than the current radical classification which originates from the 18th century.

The six writings concretely designate six classes of characters, with each Chinese character belonging to one class. Each class gathers characters that have the same structure (i.e., role and relation between the different character parts). The six classes are given below. For each class, representative characters are given.

Pictograms—象形

These characters are directly induced by the graphical representations of their meanings. The three pictogram examples 山 "mountain," 雨 "rain," and 馬 "horse" are given in Table 3.4 in the various styles described in Section 2.1 (oracle bone script, bronze, big seal, seal, and regular) to better understand the character origins.

Ideograms—指事

These characters directly indicate the position or the relation between their elements. Examples of ideograms that indicate the position include 上 "top, above" and 下 "down, below," with the wide horizontal stroke being the positional reference. Examples of ideograms that directly indicate a count include the numbers 一 "one," 二 "two," and 三 "three." Finally, examples of ideograms that combine an element to indicate a specific part of another element include 本 "root, origin" with the lower horizontal

46   *Conventional Description*

Table 3.4: Illustrating the pictogram character class.

Oracle bone	Bronze	Big seal	Seal	Regular
山	山	山	山	山
雨	雨	雨	雨	雨
馬	馬	馬	馬	馬

stroke indicating the root of the tree (木), and 末 "apex" with the upper horizontal stroke indicating the apex of the tree.

Phono-semantic compounds—形聲

These characters combine elements for their pronunciations with other elements for their meanings. Phono-semantic compounds are usually of the form radical (semantic information) + phonetic element, and are thus also known as radical-phonetic compounds. It is well-known that, and as shown in Chapter 5, the vast majority (80% to 90% depending on the dictionary considered) of characters are phono-semantic compounds. Examples of such characters include 河 "river," combining the meaning of

The six writings **47**

the radical 氵 "water" with the phonetic information of
可, and 杭 "stake (post)," combining the meaning of the
radical 木 "tree" with the phonetic information of 亢.

Compound ideographs—會意

These characters realize the combination of the meanings of their respective elements. Examples of compound
ideographs include 林 "woods" and 森 "forest," combining twice and thrice the character 木 "tree," respectively,
and the character 明 "bright," combining 日 "sun" and 月
"moon."

Phonetic loans—假借

The pronunciations of these characters have been borrowed to designate a totally different meaning. Examples of phonetic loans (a.k.a. rebus) include 來 of original meaning "wheat" and whose pronunciation (*lái* in old
Chinese, *rai* in Japanese) being close to that of the verb
"come," it is now used to express "come," and "wheat" is
now expressed with 麥 (its pronunciation having evolved
to *mài*). Another example is that of the character 要 originally "waist" and whose original pronunciation *yāo* being
close to that of the verb "want," it is now used to express
"want," and "waist" is now expressed with 腰.

Derivative cognates—轉注

Even though tentative explanations have been proposed

48 Conventional Description

(see for instance page 12 of the book by Léon Wieger "Caractères chinois" (in French), third edition, 1916), this character class remains obscure. The two derivative cognate examples given by Xú Shěn in the afterword of his *Shuōwén jiězì* dictionary are 老 and 考 (vol. 15, part 1, pp. 5–6). The original meanings of both characters can be linked to "old."

3.3 Radicals

"neck,"
"head"

For centuries (simple chronology given below), Chinese characters have been classified according to their radicals. By principle, the radical of a character corresponds to one part of the character, or to the whole character in some cases (e.g., 雨 "rain"), and should be easily identified – radicals are indeed introduced to facilitate character classification. In practice, this is not always the case, as it is sometimes difficult to identify the radical of a character, especially when a character has been subject to simplification. The radical of a character can thus remain debated. This topic is discussed in more detail in Chapter 8. Radical specification for a character can also be ambiguous, and as a result, such character classification could vary from one reference to another. For example, the radical of the character 全 is defined as 玉 by the *Kadokawa shinjigen* dictionary,[2] as 入 by the *Shinmeikai kokugo jiten* dictionary,[3] and as 人 by the online reference http://kakijun.jp.

Such classification enables facilitated character look-up inside reference books, like modern dictionaries. For comparison, where words written with the Latin alphabet are conventionally classified according to the alphabetical order, Chinese characters being a logographic script such ordering is not feasible, or at least not practical. Another classification method based on the number of strokes included in characters could be imagined, yet again is of low practicability as there are numerous characters that have the same number of strokes. Still, the stroke number is often used as a second classification criterion, that is, characters are first classified according to their radicals, and all the characters for one radical are further ordered according to their stroke numbers, typically in ascending order. For the sake of completeness, it is worth mentioning that other character classification systems have been introduced. The 四角號碼 *sìjiǎo hàomǎ* character look-up system is probably the most well-known and most used supplementary indexing method, and whose approach is to assign an integer to each element of the four corners of a character, even though there is no guarantee that each four digit sequence corresponds to one unique character. This method is also conveniently used, for

---

[2]角川 新字源, revised edition, Tokyo, Japan: Kadokawa (角川), 1994.
[3]新明解 国語辞典, fifth edition, Tokyo, Japan: Sanseido (三省堂), 1997.

50　　*Conventional Description*

Table 3.5: Examples of radicals holding the semantic information for a character.

Radical	Meaning	Sample characters
木	tree	榎 "hackberry tree," 楠 "camphor tree," 森 "forest"
魚	fish	鮫 "shark," 鯨 "whale," 鮭 "salmon," 鯉 "carp"
火	fire	灰 "ash," 燃 "burn," 煙 "smoke," 焼 "grill"
水 (氵)	water	氷 "ice," 汗 "sweat," 池 "pond," 涙 "tear," 泣 "cry"

example, to look-up Tangut characters (see Figure 2.4).

As explained in the previous section, a majority of Chinese characters are phono-semantic compounds (a.k.a. radical-phonetic compounds). The radical of a character thus very often holds the semantic information of characters. Several examples are given in Table 3.5.

The usage of radicals for Chinese character classification can be traced back to the already mentioned 2nd century dictionary *Shuōwén jiězì* (説文解字) by Xú Shěn. In this ancient manuscript, Chinese characters are classified according to 540

Pronunciation   51

radicals. This early classification system was superseded by that of the *Zihuì* dictionary (字彙), which was compiled during the Ming dynasty by Mei Yingzuo and distributed in 1615. The *Zihuì* dictionary reduced the number of radicals from 540 to 214, which is the radical list still in use today. The modern list of character radicals thus includes these 214 elements, which were denoted as 部首 for the first time in the 18th century *Kāngxī* dictionary (康熙字典).

The currently used 214 radicals are listed in Table 3.6. Radicals are conventionally ordered by number of strokes. Note that some radicals have variants, which appear in this table on the right side of the radical with a smaller font size (e.g., イ is a variant of the radical 人). The admitted radical variants may differ from one reference to another, thus further increasing classification ambiguity. We abide by the *Kadokawa shinjigen* dictionary (although we ignore differences induced by font design only).

3.4   Pronunciation

First, we focus on the cases of Chinese and Korean. In Chinese, by principle, each character has one single pronunciation, even though the pronunciation of a character is subject to fluctuations when considering different Chinese dialects (e.g., Mandarin and Cantonese). Moreover, two characters may share the same pronunciation. For instance, in Mandarin Chinese, the characters

52   *Conventional Description*

Table 3.6: The conventional 214 Chinese character radicals.

Strokes	Radicals	Count
1	一丨丶丿乙亅	6
2	二亠人亻儿入八冂冖冫几凵刀刂力勹匕匚匸十卜卩㔾厂厶又	23
3	口囗土士夂夊夕大女子宀寸小⺌尢尣兀尸屮山巛巜川工己巾干幺广廴廾弋弓彐彑彐彡彳	31
4	心忄㣺戈戶手扌支攴攵文斗斤方无旡日曰月木欠止歹殳毋比毛氏气水氵氺火灬爪爫父爻爿片牙牛牜犬犭	34
5	玄玉王瓜瓦甘生用田疋⺪疒癶白皮皿目罒矛矢石示礻禸禾穴立	23
6	竹米糸缶网罒罓罒羊⺶⺷羽老耂而耒耳聿肉月臣自至臼舌舛舟艮色艸艹虍虫血行衣衤襾西	29
7	見角言谷豆豕豸貝赤走足⻊身車辛辰辵辶辶邑⻏酉釆里	20
8	金長門阜⻖隶隹雨青靑非	9
9	面革韋韭音頁風飛食飠首香	11
10	馬骨高髟鬥鬯鬲鬼	8
11	魚鳥鹵鹿麥麦麻	6
12	黃黄黍黑黒黹	4
13	黽鼎鼓鼠	4
14	鼻齊斉	2
15	齒齒	1
16	龍竜龜	2
17	龠	1
	Total	214

糖 and 塘 are both pronounced *táng*, and the characters 倘 and 淌 are both pronounced *tǎng*. In Korean, Chinese characters (*hanja*) have by principle, as in Chinese, one unique pronunciation. For example, the character 人 is read *in*, 大 *dae*, and 小 *so*. Although language natural evolution tends to further set Chinese and Korean apart, because sharing the same roots, pronunciation similarities can still be noticed between these two languages.

"read," "interpret"

Next, we look at the case of Annamese (Vietnamese). A Chinese character as used in Annamese (Chữ nôm) may have different readings: for example, the character 常 may be read *xàng* that is directly after the Chinese reading, and retaining the original meaning. Or, the character 常 can also be borrowed from Chinese to write a Vietnamese word with a similar meaning; for instance, to write the word *thường* "often." As another example, one can cite the character 本, which may be read *bản* after Chinese, or, borrowed to write the Vietnamese word *vốn* "capital." As a result, several different readings can exist for one character. However, such examples remain rather infrequent, and it is commonly admitted that just as for Chinese and Korean, a Chinese character in Annamese has one pronunciation. As previously noted, two distinct characters can share the same pronunciation, for example 剛 and 鋼 are both *gang*. Finally, as presented in Chapter 2, Chữ nôm has local characters, most of them being phono-semantic

54   *Conventional Description*

compounds, that is a character made of two parts, one bearing the Annamese pronunciation information, derived from the Chinese original reading, and the other the semantic information, derived from the original character meaning.

Because based on the "one character, one pronunciation" principle, the pronunciation of Chinese characters in the cases of Chinese, Korean, and Annamese is rather simple from a logical point of view.

The case of Japanese is significantly more complex. Effectively, character readings can be split into two main categories: the *kun* (訓) readings and the *on* (音) readings. The former refers to Japanese specific pronunciation, that is, to the Japanese language as it was even before Chinese characters were in use within it. The latter refer to readings derived directly from Chinese. Yet, it is important to note that the Chinese language itself had several different readings for a same character depending, for instance, on the time period considered. It is also important to note that Chinese pronunciation could not be reused as is in Japanese as the language phonemes are different. Still, *on* readings are easily linked to the Chinese pronunciations of a character, that is minding some sound adjustments.

The *on* readings of a character in Japanese are further split into several categories depending on the Chinese pronunciation sort that was used to obtain the current *on* reading. Three *on* readings are conventionally distinguished: *go-on* (呉音), *kan-on* (漢音), and *tō-on* (唐音, sometimes called *sō-on* (宋音) or *tōsō-on* (唐宋音)), in chronological order of their appearance. All three sorts of readings may not remain for all characters. In fact, the *tō-on* reading is known for very few characters, mostly characters that are related to the Buddhist sect Zen. Moreover, a character may have the same *go-on* and *kan-on* readings.

The earliest *on* reading sort that made it to Japan, *go-on*, seems to have originated from a southern Chinese dialect south of the Yangtze river during the Six Dynasties. The phonetic properties of *go-on* include the distinction of voiced and unvoiced consonants such as /t/ and /d/, and the conservation of the original Chinese nasal sounds /m/ and /n/. The *go-on* reading is especially used for Buddhism-related terms.

The next in time *on* reading sort, *kan-on*, originates from a northern Chinese dialect (by opposition to *go-on*, which relates to a southern dialect) of the Tang dynasty in the area of the actual Xi'an and Luoyang cities. The main differences with *go-on* include the usage of unvoiced consonants in place of voiced ones such as /z/, /d/, and /b/ (/s/, /t/, and /f/ used instead), the original nasal sounds /m/ and /n/ become the voiced /b/ and /d/, and the suffixed /t/ becomes /tsu/ when it was /tchi/ with *go-on*.

The following *on* reading sort, *tō-on*, originates from the Chinese of the Song dynasty (宋 *sō*, hence the other names *sō-on* or *tōsō-on* for this reading sort) in the Jiangnan, Zhejiang, and Nanjing area. It reached Japan through trade and religious (mainly the Buddhist sect Zen) matters in the Middle ages (thus entering the country mostly from Nagasaki). Only a few words

56   *Conventional Description*

Table 3.7: Examples illustrating the three main *on* readings of the Japanese language.

Character	行	和
go-on	*gyō*	*wa*
	(e.g., 行書 *gyō-sho*)	(e.g., 和鳴 *wa-mei*)
kan-on	*kō*	*ka*
	(e.g., 平行 *hei-kō*)	(e.g., 和鸞 *ka-ran*)
tō-on	*an, hin*	*o*
	(e.g., 行燈 *an-don*)	(e.g., 和尚 *o-shō*)

remain with a *tō-on* reading. Examples illustrating these three main *on* readings are given in Table 3.7.

Finally, it is worth noting that in addition to *kun* and *on* readings, a third character reading sort specific to Japanese, *ko-on* (古音), preceding the others, has been witnessed by linguists and historians. However, very few details of this reading are known, including its geographical origins. Examples of *ko-on* readings include 宜 *ga*, 里 *ro*, and 意 *o*.

On a side note, let us recall that *kokuji* characters as previously presented in Section 2.4 almost only have *kun* readings. This can be easily understood by recalling that *kokuji* characters are local to Japan, thus not holding Chinese roots and therefore having no *on* reading. There are some exceptions, though, with

Pronunciation 57

a few *kokuji* characters having only *on* readings, and even more infrequent, *kokuji* characters holding both *on* and *kun* readings (refer to Table 2.6 for details and examples).

To conclude this section on character pronunciation, we note that traditionally, Japanese has also relied on the pronunciations, *kun* or *on*, of some Chinese characters to phonetically write words (Pattern 1). These are often foreign words (loanwords), but not exclusively. The reverse is also happening: the character readings are ignored, the character meanings being solely retained (Pattern 2). Such words are most of the time loanwords. In either of these two usage patterns, such characters are called *ateji*. Even though minor due to the relatively rare occurrences of *ateji*-based words, this is thus another difficulty when reading Chinese characters in Japanese: in Pattern 1, they might be used as phonetic symbols with readings that are more or less close to the regular *kun* and *on* readings, or worse in Pattern 2 used as semantic symbols with exotic readings (loanwords). In the first pattern, the character meanings are irrelevant or almost irrelevant. Common examples of words written with *ateji* characters in Pattern 1 include 寿司 *sushi* "sushi," 目出度い *medetai* "felicitous" for native Japanese words, and 仏蘭西 *furansu* "France," 珈琲 *kōhī* "coffee" for loanwords. Examples for Pattern 2 include 頁 "page," 庭球 "tennis" (literally "garden ball"), and 緑玉 "emerald" (literally "green gem"), both read directly in English. The usage of *ateji* characters is declining though, with the *katakana* script being commonly used instead. In the

58   *Conventional Description*

case of Chinese, transcription of foreign words is performed according to the official standard maintained by the public Xinhua News Agency. Transcription in Chinese can rely either on phonetic (e.g., 安東尼 *āndōngní* "Antoine, Anthony" as in 馬克安東尼 "Marcus Antonius"), semantic information (e.g., 美國 *měiguó* "United States," literally "beautiful country"), or both (e.g., 可口可樂 *kěkǒukělè* "Coca Cola," literally "tasty, enjoyable") for a character. However, unlike Japanese, transcriptions remain easy to read in Chinese thanks to the "one character, one pronunciation" principle. Transcriptions of foreign words with Chinese characters are sometimes shared between Japanese and Chinese (e.g., 英國 "United Kingdom"), the readings remaining distinct though.

3.5   Terminology

In this section, specialized terms used in the book are presented and, if needed, discussed and justified.

"word,"
"expression"

The terms ideogram and pictogram were explained and illustrated when presenting character classification according to the six writings (see Section 3.2). Hence, a Chinese character can be either an ideogram or a pictogram, but it can also be neither, remember, for instance, the phono-semantic compounds. As a result, it is necessary

Terminology   59

to rely on another term to designate Chinese characters in general. The word "logogram" is commonly accepted. Yet, the reader should note that this is a much-debated topic.

Even though not terminology strictly speaking, orthodox character forms are used as much as possible in this book to retain a global point of view. In fact, character simplifications are most of the time specific to one language or dialect.

In addition, Chinese characters are often referred to as *kanji* (*hànzì* in Chinese), which is the common Japanese appellation for Chinese characters. The name 漢字 *kanji* literally means "Han character," with "Han" in the sense of China's Han dynasty (206 B.C.–220 A.D.). Even though common, and rather convenient, this appellation is avoided in this book for the simple reason that, as presented for instance in Chapter 2, the characters addressed here are not all Han characters. Effectively, almost all languages and dialects relying on Chinese characters have introduced additional, local characters that are specific to the language. This is the case, for instance, of Japanese's *kokuji* and Korean's *gukja* characters. Hence, the *kanji* appellation will not be used here. Besides, it could well be argued that the same issue holds for the "Chinese character" appellation, as local characters are not Chinese ones. Yet, even if not 100% Chinese, such local characters consist of elements that are themselves 100% Chinese characters. Therefore, for the sake of conciseness and readability, the "Chinese character" appellation is used in this book, but the even more restrictive – and language

60   *Conventional Description*

dependent – *kanji* name is not.

Finally, as presented in Section 3.3, Chinese characters are commonly classified according to radicals, such as inside dictionaries. The term "radical," whose etymology indicates the meaning of "root," may be subject to discussion. For example, in French, the term "radical" with respect to a Chinese character is translated as *clef* "key", and not as *radical* "radical." The radical of a Chinese character corresponds to the Chinese word 部首, literally "section header" – see, for instance, the definition in the *Kōjien* Japanese dictionary[4] – in the sense that a Chinese character dictionary consists of characters classified under several sections. So, one should first note that the word "radical" is not the literal translation of the corresponding Chinese term (部首). Such a section of a character dictionary is distinguished by a radical and denoted, for instance, by 口部 for the radical 口 "mouth."

In the author's opinion, the term "radical" (i.e., from "root") bears the meaning of the "vital, essential, master" element. From an *ideogram* point of view, it is indeed right to consider the radical the most important element of the character. However, it is critical to recall that Chinese characters are *not* all ideograms – indeed just a small fraction are – instead Chinese characters are logograms. Hence, it does not make much sense to assign to the element that holds the semantic information the

---

[4]広辞苑, Tokyo, Japan: Iwanami Shoten (岩波書店), 2008.

Terminology   61

master role. The element that holds for instance the phonetic information is just as important. Therefore, the author prefers the term "key," as in the general computer science sense, to designate the information that is used to classify an object. In other words, for Chinese characters the term "key" designates the element that is used to classify the character, and that is all. This term does not imply anything about the importance of the element. As a result, the author thinks that the term "key" is more appropriate than "radical" when dealing with Chinese characters in general, that is, not only with ideograms. Coulmas, in his book "The writing systems of the world," seems to think similarly but uses the term "classifier" instead of "key." In spite of this opinion, for the sake of clarity, and especially with respect to related works, the term "radical" will be used in this book to stay in accordance with the convention.

Finally, it should be noted that some authors such as Léon Wieger assign to the term "radical" yet another meaning: an element of a character that simply has its own meaning, and which can thus be composed by several sub-elements (in later chapters, we would say that a radical in this specific sense is not necessarily a canonical element).

62   *Conventional Description*

Bibliographical notes

1. The *Shuōwén jiězì* (説文解字, *Setsumon kaiji* in Japanese) dictionary is an ancient work from the 2nd century. It introduces a now defunct character classification system based on 540 radicals, compared with the "modern" system of 214. This dictionary notably conducts character analysis, distinguishing, for example, character compounds from others. Reprints are still widely available, with, for instance, 説文解字注 (Shanghai, China: Shanghai Guji Chubanshe (上海古籍出版社), 1981).

2. Being often considered as the origin of the radical system still in use today when dealing with Chinese characters, the *Kāngxī* dictionary (康熙字典, *Kōki jiten* in Japanese) is well-known in the field. This 18th century dictionary is the reference for character forms as used in traditional Chinese, Korean (*hanja*), and Japanese (at the exception of simplified forms). Reprints are still available, with, for instance, 康熙字典 (Beijing, China: Zhonghua Book Company (中華書局), 2009).

3. In French, the early occidental reference work by Léon Wieger "Caractères chinois" (third edition, 1916) conducts a broad review – more in the form of an encyclopedia rather than that of a conventional dictionary – of vari-

Bibliographical notes   63

ous aspects of Chinese characters, including etymological aspects, phonetic ones for the Chinese language, and historic roots of characters (oracle bone script). These are notably reviewed through several historic texts from the first three Chinese dynasties (the Xia, Shang, and Zhou dynasties).

64   *Conventional Description*

CHAPTER 4

Character Relations

In this chapter, several relations defined between Chinese characters will be presented. Such relations are applicable to any Chinese character. Yet, it is often more meaningful with respect to applications to restrict the set of the considered characters to one that suits the selected application. For example, it is difficult, and probably of low merit, to identify exhaustively all the characters in relation with another one. Concretely, in the case of a pedagogic application, it would be meaningful for the teacher to first select a set of Chinese characters to be remembered by his students and then to derive relations among the characters of this particular set.

4.1 Notations and definitions

"record,"
"writing"

Since Chinese characters are approached hereinafter from a scientific point of view, several basic notations and definitions will first be recalled. As graphs provide some theoretical basis in this chapter, we will focus in this section on graph-related definitions.

A graph $G = (V, E)$ consists of a set of nodes (a.k.a. vertices) V and a set of edges $E \subseteq V \times V$. A graph can be either directed (a.k.a. a digraph), in which case the two edges (u, v) and (v, u) are distinct ($\forall u, v \in V, u \neq v$), or undirected, in which case the two edges (u, v) and (v, u) are identical ($\forall u, v \in V$). The set of nodes of a graph G is also conveniently denoted by $V(G)$, that is, using the operator $V()$ (whose name is unrelated to that of the node set), and similarly $E(G)$ for the set of edges. Not only nodes but also edges can be valued: a value is thus assigned to a node or edge. Besides, a graph can have double edges. In this case, edges can be distinguished according to some edge property (e.g., edge type).

The order of a graph G is its number of nodes, that is $|V(G)|$.

Notations and definitions   67

The degree $d_G(u)$ of a node $u \in V(G)$ is the number of edges at u. In other words, the degree of u is the number of neighbor nodes of u. The degree $d(G)$ of G is the average degree of all its nodes. A path in a graph is an alternate sequence of nodes and edges, started and ended by two end (a.k.a. terminal) nodes. In the case of a digraph, the edges included in a path obviously all go in the same direction.

In addition, a few logic symbols are used hereinafter: equivalence is denoted by $\Leftrightarrow$, implication by $\Rightarrow$ (or $\Leftarrow$), negation (NOT; a.k.a. logical complement) by $\neg$, and logical conjunction (AND) by $\wedge$. The other notations used are common mathematical ones and are thus not detailed here.

Finally, a binary relation is formally defined as follows. A relation R between a set X and a set Y is specified by a subset E of the Cartesian product $X \times Y$. For two elements $x \in X$ and $y \in Y$, the statement "x is related to y with respect to R" holds if and only if $(x,y) \in E$. If this condition is satisfied, the relation is denoted by xRy (or alternatively $R(x,y)$). It should be noted that relations are not necessarily symmetric: xRy is not the same as yRx. For example, the binary relation $=$ on integers is symmetric: $i = j \Leftrightarrow j = i$, but the binary relation $<$ is not: $i < j \not\Leftrightarrow j < i$ (in this case, the $<$ relation is said to be asymmetric).

4.2 Morphological relations

Interestingly, Chinese characters frequently have a recursive structure: a Chinese character often consists of several Chinese characters. Hence, a Chinese character can often be decomposed into several others. The characters that do not bend to this rule are said to be canonical: comparable to prime numbers in mathematics, they cannot be further decomposed. Canonical characters thus usually have few strokes: 日 "day," 口 "mouth," and 月 "moon" are some examples. While still rather imprecise, character decomposition, including canonical characters, will be formally discussed in Chapter 5.

4.2.1 Ancestor-child relations

"shape": 开 and 彡

The two character relations "is child of" and "is ancestor of" are defined below. These definitions rely on the character inclusion principle. Again, this morphological aspect will be formally defined in Chapter 5. For now, character inclusion is defined informally as follows: a character u is included in a character v if and only if u appears inside v. For example, the character 木 is included inside the character 椿 as it appears on its left side.

Definition 1. *For a Chinese character u, a character v is a* child *for u if and only if $u \neq v$ and v includes u as a sub-character.*

Morphological relations 69

And, conversely:

Definition 2. *For a Chinese character u, a character v is an* ancestor *for u if and only if u ≠ v and u includes v as a sub-character.*

For example, the character 丘 "hill" is included inside the character 兵 "soldier." So, the character 丘 is an ancestor for 兵, and conversely, the character 兵 is a child for 丘. With only these two relations defined, it is already possible to obtain a cartography of Chinese characters. A sample illustration is given in Figure 4.1.

The following properties can be deduced directly from Definition 1.

Property 1. *The child relation is irreflexive: for u any character, $\neg(uRu)$ holds, with R the child relation.*

This is indeed trivial from the definition: $u \neq v$ is a necessary condition.

Property 2. *The child relation is antisymmetric: for u, v any two characters, $(uRv) \wedge (u \neq v)$ implies that $\neg(vRu)$ holds, with R the child relation.*

This is also trivial: in general, a container cannot be the content of its content.

As a result, these two properties induce the following third property.

Character Relations

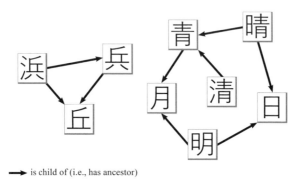

→ is child of (i.e., has ancestor)

Figure 4.1: Illustrating the child and ancestor morphological relations between Chinese characters.

Property 3. *The child relation is asymmetric: for u,v any two characters, $uRv \Rightarrow \neg(vRu)$, with R the child relation.*

From Definition 2, the same properties can be also deduced for the ancestor relation. That is, the ancestor relation is irreflexive, antisymmetric, and therefore asymmetric.

4.2.2 Deriving layers and learning paths

As mentioned in the introduction of this chapter, it is most of the time more meaningful to consider a restricted set of characters

Morphological relations 71

and to discuss their relations, rather than considering the set of all the Chinese characters. An important application is Chinese character memorization. Character relations can support memorization by the learner, an important role of the teacher being to assemble sets of characters along his course.

By arranging the characters into layers, say vertical ones, such that 1) there is at most one path between any two characters and 2) all links are forward, that is, there is no link inside one same layer nor one going to a lower layer, it is possible to derive learning paths. A learning path suggests to the learner an efficient way to memorize a character by learning successively the characters on the path until reaching the terminal one. Even though it depends on the considered character set, learning paths would often start from canonical characters. Moreover, it is interesting to note that such layers and learning paths are dynamic in the sense that they may evolve depending on the considered character set. Effectively, adding or removing characters could impact layers and learning paths. As an example, characters organized into vertical layers are illustrated in Figure 4.2, with the first layer (Layer 1) containing canonical characters. One should note that the bottom-most two characters in Layer 1 are distinct: they are the character 口 "mouth" and the radical 囗, as presented in Chapter 3.

From this organization into layers, it is possible to deduce the learning paths 月 → 青 → 晴 and 日 → 晴 to support the memorization of the character 晴 "sunny."

72 *Character Relations*

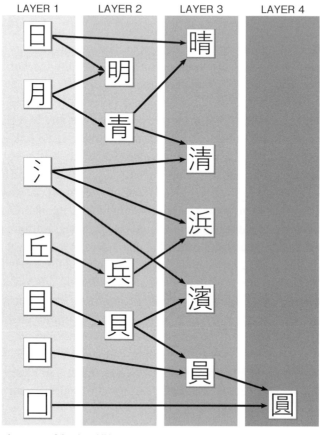

→ is ancestor of (i.e., has child)

Figure 4.2: Deriving layers and learning paths from ancestor-child relations.

4.3 Semantic relations

"form,"
"body"

To not confuse the reader, we have purposefully omitted to mention a particularity of Chinese characters in Chapter 3: Chinese characters very often have variants. In other words, a single character often has several different possible writings. To further refine this difficult to define aspect, one character, in the sense of "meaning" (i.e., we could here use the term "ideogram"), often has variants, in the sense of "writing," "shape": the character, in the sense of "meaning," remains untouched, but its rendering may be altered. We can thus propose the following definition.

Definition 3. *For a Chinese character u, a character v is a variant of u if and only if v is a different writing of u.*

And, we can derive the following two properties.

Property 4. *The variant relation is irreflexive: for u any character, $\neg(uRu)$ holds, with R the variant relation.*

This can be directly deduced from Definition 3.

Property 5. *The variant relation is symmetric: for u, v any two characters, $uRv \Leftrightarrow vRu$, with R the variant relation.*

Obviously, if a character u is a variant of a character v, then v is also a variant of u. Several examples of character variants

74   *Character Relations*

have been already given in Chapter 2, for instance in Table 2.1; more will be given below.

There exist several sorts of variants. We speak of *forms*. Yet, due to a lack of standardization, the form names given to the different character variants vary from one language to another. For instance, simplified Chinese, traditional Chinese, and Japanese sometimes name the forms of character variants differently. These differences remain rather infrequent, so, minding possible slight variations, we detail the main different character forms in the rest of this section. Examples are selected from the mainstream *Kadokawa shinjigen* dictionary unless stated otherwise.

orthodox form—舊字

> The orthodox form usually refers to the character variant that has been stable since the Northern and Southern dynasties (420–589) and which thus made it into the *Kāngxī* dictionary. Note that the orthodox form is sometimes referred to as 正字 *seiji*, literally the "correct form," as for example in the *Ganlu zishu*, but as detailed later in this section, this appellation will not be used in this book.
>
> When opposing the orthodox form to the simplified form, it is common to refer to the old form and to the new form, respectively. This old–new form distinction is typically found in languages that underwent character simplification, such as simplified Chinese and Japanese. On a side

Semantic relations   75

note, Chinese characters used in Korean are usually orthodox forms.

new form—新字

As with the old form, the new form is defined and typically used within languages that underwent character simplification, that is opposing for a character the new, simplified form to the traditional, non-simplified one. Hence,
the new form of a character in simplified Chinese and in
Japanese is likely to be different as the simplification reforms were conducted independently. In Table 4.1 are
illustrated new forms that are different in Chinese and Japanese.

Table 4.1: Illustrating new and old forms in the cases of simplified Chinese
and Japanese.

Old form	對	獸	醬	勸	堯
New form (Chinese)	对	兽	酱	劝	尧
New form (Japanese)	対	獣	醤	勧	堯

vulgar form—俗字

Vulgar form characters (in the classical sense of "vulgate"
and not that of "rude") correspond to frequent, yet unofficial simplifications made by people when writing. Thus,
the vulgar form should not be confused with the new (sim-

76   *Character Relations*

plified) form. The reasons behind the appearance of vulgar forms might be for instance the high difficulty of the original character (e.g., the difficulty induced by a high number of strokes), or simply calligraphic mistakes. The locally simplified characters, as introduced in Section 2.4, are, in some cases, considered vulgar forms. Some differences can arise depending on the language: a character variant can be deemed vulgar by one and a new form by another.

First, examples of vulgar forms in the case of Japanese are given in Table 4.2, the orthodox and original forms being given for reference. In addition, relying on the 7th–8th century *Ganlu zishu* dictionary, we give in Table 4.3 vulgar forms in the case of Chinese, from a Tang dynasty point of view (618–907).

Table 4.2: Examples of vulgar form characters in the case of Japanese. The original form is also given for reference.

Orthodox form	嫂	學	杯	毘	浸
Original form	㛮	斅	桮	毗	濅
Vulgar form	娵	㝏	柸	毗	浸

original form—本字

The original form of a character is sometimes used to ex-

Table 4.3: Examples of vulgar form characters in the case of Tang dynasty (618–907) Chinese.

Orthodox form	功	兜	澌	耆	鴎
Vulgar form	功	兊	澌	耆	鵶

plain its semantic roots or its current morphology. A character in the old form may have differences, and not only minor ones, with its original form variant. Several character differences between the old form and the original form (with respect to Japanese) are illustrated in Table 4.4.

Table 4.4: Illustrating differences between the old and original forms in Japanese. The new form is given for reference.

Original form	鋪	斷	晉	彊	从
Old form	舖	斷	晉	彌	從
New form	舗	断	晋	弥	従

ancient form—古字

The ancient form of a character refers to an early variant, for instance as found in the 2nd century *Shuōwén jiězì* dictionary, or in even earlier Chinese bronze inscriptions. The ancient form of a character may have no or almost no

78   *Character Relations*

relation with the original form of the character.

We give in Table 4.5 several examples of characters that illustrate differences between the ancient form and the original form (the old form is assimilated to the original form, as no distinct character variant for the original form is known to the author). Once again, for comparison, we have selected characters whose new (with respect to Japanese), old, and ancient forms are distinct.

Table 4.5: Illustrating differences between the ancient and original forms. New forms (with respect to Japanese) are given for reference.

Ancient form	昚	礼	帰	气	銕
Original form*	愼	禮	歸	氣	鐵
New form	慎	礼	帰	気	鉄

* Old form assimilated to the original form as explained.

erroneous form—誤字

While the vulgar form is, or had been, tolerated, the erroneous form of a character is clearly recognized as a mistake. The erroneous form of a character thus designates a character variant specified by the same mistake that has been attested several times. Several examples of erroneous forms are presented in Table 4.6 with the corresponding orthodox forms.

Table 4.6: Examples of erroneous forms.

Orthodox form	僭	羲	叫	寧	恤
Erroneous form	僣	羲	呌	寗	䘏

alternative form

There exist some characters that have variants that do not fall into one of the previous form categories or for which it is too difficult to state a suitable category. We thus often speak (in Japanese) of *bettaiji* (別體字), namely, the "alternative form." Examples of alternative forms are given in Table 4.7, with both the orthodox and original forms provided for comparison.

Table 4.7: Examples of alternative forms. The orthodox and original forms are given for reference.

Orthodox form	跬	卉	島	弼	徇
Original form	趌	芔	㠀	弻	𢓜
Alternative form	蹞	卉	嶋	弼	侚

Finally, we return to the *correct form* (正字) of a character as briefly mentioned earlier. The definition of this character vari-

80   *Character Relations*

ant remains rather vague. Indeed, the name of this form literally means "correct character." Thus, the "correct form" appellation sometimes stands for the orthodox form of a character and sometimes for the character variant that is officially endorsed by the local authorities. This appellation is thus ambiguous as, depending on, say, the editor, it may designate distinct variants of a same character, as illustrated previously.

To conclude this topic on character forms, it is worth mentioning that some characters may be represented with a certain degree of stylistic difference and that especially across different languages (e.g., Chinese, Japanese, Korean style differences). Nonetheless, characters featuring such cosmetic changes should not be mistaken for character variants, even though it is often difficult to be assertive when differentiating character cosmetic changes from character variants. Mitsuo Fukawa and Kazuo Koike presented their opinion on this issue in their book "Introduction to old *kanji* and old *kana*."[1] Several examples that illustrate such character cosmetic changes are given in Table 4.8. Fukawa and Koike also give character pairs that feature cosmetic changes such as those of the pairs 雪, 雪 and 高, 髙. Yet, these slight character variations are considered as proper character variants by, for instance, the *Kadokawa shinjigen* dictionary, precisely 雪 being mentioned as the old form of 雪, and 髙 being

---

[1]旧字旧かな入門 (in Japanese), Tokyo, Japan: Kashiwashobo (柏書房), 2001.

Semantic relations   81

mentioned as the vulgar form of 高. Further, one should note that even if barely noticeable, character cosmetic changes may involve slightly different strokes. For example, the first stroke of the character 視 (i.e., the dot stroke) is rendered differently when writing this character as 視. Precisely, the first stroke remains the dot stroke but a different type of dot. (Indeed, four types of the dot stroke are commonly distinguished, including for instance the reversed dot.)

Table 4.8: Examples of characters written differently by means of cosmetic changes.

Style 1	戶	言	紅	令	鳩
Style 2	户	言	紅	令	鳩*

* Given as a character variant in the Daikanwa jiten dictionary (see Chapter 9), but not in the Kadokawa shinjigen.

Next, semantic relations can be derived, in other words, putting into relation any two characters that are variants to each other, according to the character variants defined previously. Here, it is important to note that a character may have several variants of the same form, for example two different ancient forms. The locally simplified characters as presented in Section 2.4 also fall into the semantic relation category. Figure 4.3 illustrates various semantic relations between several characters,

Character Relations

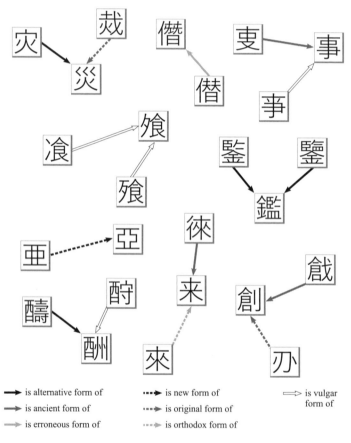

Figure 4.3: Examples of semantic relations between Chinese characters.

Morpho-semantic relations 83

notably with, as mentioned previously, several variants of the same form for one single character.

We now specify the properties of these form relations. When refining the variant relation down to the form level, the symmetry property no longer holds. Instead, the following properties hold:

Property 6. *The form relation is irreflexive: for u any character, $\neg(uRu)$ holds, with R a form relation.*

Proof. For u, v any two characters, $uRv \Rightarrow uR'v$ holds, with R a form relation and R' the variant relation. Since R' is irreflexive, R is irreflexive. $\square$

Property 7. *The form relation is asymmetric: for u, v any two characters, $uRv \Rightarrow \neg(vRu)$, with R a form relation.*

Obviously, if a character u is a form, say $\mathscr{F}$, of a character v (e.g., $\mathscr{F}$ stands for *ancient form*), then uRv with R the form relation with respect to $\mathscr{F}$ is satisfied. However, the opposite does not hold: v is not a form $\mathscr{F}$ of u.

4.4 Morpho-semantic relations

Borrowing aspects of both morphological and semantic relations, we call the radical relation morpho-semantic. This is the only relation we define in this category.

84 *Character Relations*

As detailed in Chapter 2, each Chinese character has one unique radical, and the radical often holds semantic information for the character, while the remaining part of the character often holds phonetic information. Hence, there is a hybrid aspect to this relation: on the one hand, two characters having the same radical are very likely to include the radical as a common element, thus inducing a morphological relation, and on the other hand, two characters having the same radical are very likely to share the meaning conveyed by the radical, thus inducing a semantic relation.

"cedar," the beautiful tree

As an example, consider the two characters 松 "pine [tree]" and 杉 "cedar," which are both of radical 木 "tree." These two characters are thus in morpho-semantic relation. The morphological aspect of this relation is obvious: both characters 松 and 杉 have, on their left sides, the radical 木.

In other words, and to reuse the terminology introduced previously, the two characters 松 and 杉 are children of the character 木, and conversely, the character 木 is an ancestor of both characters 松 and 杉. Next, the semantic aspect of the morpho-semantic relation between 松 and 杉 is similarly obvious: both characters' meanings, namely "pine [tree]" and "cedar," directly involve the meaning of their radical, namely "tree."

Next, let us consider the algebraic and topological properties of the radical relation. First, because a radical may have

Morpho-semantic relations   85

variants (see Chapters 2 and 6), it is necessary, when consider-ing a radical, to set the unique character representing this rad-ical, to retain the radical uniqueness property of any character. For example, we select the character 水 to represent the radical "water," which has for variants 水, 氵, and 氺.

Property 8. *The radical relation is neither reflexive nor irreflex-ive.*

Proof. While the radical of the character 水 is itself, that is 水 R 水 with R the radical relation, the radical of the character 榎 is 木 (it is recalled that a character has one unique radical).   □

Property 9. *The radical relation is antisymmetric: for u, v any two characters, $(uRv) \wedge (vRu)$ implies u and v are the same character, with R the radical relation.*

Obviously, for u, v any two distinct characters, if u is the radical of v, then, since u and v distinct, v cannot be the radical of u.

Furthermore, it is interesting to note that the graph induced, with respect to the radical relation, by the character set $C \cup \{r\}$ with C a set of characters of same radical r, and $r \notin C$, is a star. In other words, each node of C has degree 1, and the node r has degree $|C|$. An illustration of the case $C = \{栗, 杉, 松\}$ and $r = 木$ is given in Figure 4.4.

Now, we discuss some particularities of this morpho-se-mantic relation.

86   *Character Relations*

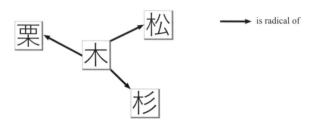

Figure 4.4: Illustrating the radical relation: a star is induced.

First, it should be noted that even though two characters of the same radical are in morpho-semantic relation as explained previously, the morphological aspect of this relation may be relegated to the background in the case where, for instance, each of the two characters has a different variant of the radical. For example, the two characters 沖 "open sea" and 泉 "[water] spring" both have 水 "water" as radical, yet this radical is of the form 氵 for the character 沖 and of the form 水 for the character 泉.

Next, the semantic aspect of this morpho-semantic relation may also be subject to relegation. This is typically the case where, for instance, one of the two characters in relation is of the pictogram class (see Chapter 3), thus with no semantic information induced by its radical. For example, we consider the two characters 呂 "backbone" and 味 "taste," both of radical

口 "mouth." The character 呂 is of the pictogram class and effectively receives no semantic information from its radical. On the contrary, the radical 口 "mouth" induces obvious semantic information to the character 味 "taste."

However, in the end, the aforementioned two situations remain rare, and it is thus sound to speak of *morpho-semantic* relation when it comes to the radical relation.

4.5 Phonetic relations

"sound,"
"tone"

It is recalled that Chinese characters have various readings, sometimes even within one language. For example, a Chinese character as used in Japanese almost always has at least one *kun* reading and at least one *on* reading, but often more. Precisely, there are several types of *on* readings: *go-on*, *kan-on*, and *tō-on*. In this section, the Chinese, Korean, Annamese, and Japanese languages are addressed in this order, reflecting the increasing complexity of phonetic relations. Before detailing phonetic relations, the following shared property is stated.

Property 10. *The phonetic relations defined below are reflexive, symmetric, and transitive: for u, v, w any three characters, uRu, $uRv \Leftrightarrow vRu$, and $(uRv) \wedge (vRw) \Rightarrow uRw$ hold, with R a phonetic relation.*

88   *Character Relations*

4.5.1   Chinese and Korean

First, let us consider the rather simple cases (at least from the pronunciation point of view) of Chinese and Korean. As explained in Chapter 3, in Chinese and Korean (*hanja*), each Chinese character has one single reading (when considering a single dialect, of course). Without loss of generality, the discussion conducted here is based on the Mandarin dialect of Chinese. From this fact, the following property with respect to Chinese can be derived.

Property 11. *The function from the set of Chinese characters onto the set of Chinese syllables that associates a character to its reading is surjective and not injective.*

Obviously, because two Chinese characters may have the same reading (see the *táng* example given in Chapter 3), the function is not injective and thus not bijective. This surjective principle for Chinese characters is known as the 一字一音 principle, literally "one character, one sound."

It is not trivial to state the same property for Korean. Indeed, because Korean is now mainly based on the Hangul writing system, it is not obvious that each syllable of modern Korean corresponds to at least one *hanja* (i.e., Chinese) character. However, this may have been the case for Korean before the introduction of Hangul in the 15th century (and possibly even until the 19th century, since the broad adoption of Hangul dates back to the

Phonetic relations 89

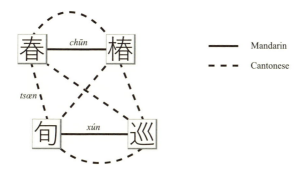

Figure 4.5: Illustrating phonetic relations between characters of different Chinese dialects.

late 19th and early 20th century).

An interesting aspect of Chinese is the presence of numerous languages (sometimes called dialects), each inducing different character readings more or less similar to each other. Mandarin, Hong-Kong's Cantonese, and Taiwan's Hokkien can be cited as Chinese dialects. Examples of induced phonetic relations are given in Figure 4.5. In this figure, we rely on valued edges so as to indicate the character reading that links two characters. In addition, several edge values are abbreviated since they are deducible from others.

90   *Character Relations*

4.5.2 Annamese

Next, we address the case of Annamese (Vietnamese's Chữ nôm script). As detailed in Chapter 3, a Chinese character may have several different readings in Annamese. Moreover, in Annamese, a Chinese character may be used for its original (Chinese) pronunciation, original meaning, or both. Finally, Chữ nôm has local characters comparable to Japanese's *kokuji* and whose readings are thus those of the corresponding Annamese words. Hence, the following four types of phonetic relations can be induced.

Type A These phonetic relations connect characters that have in common their readings that derive directly from the original Chinese ones, and that also retain the original character meanings. In other words, the meaning of the Annamese word corresponding to the reading is the same as the original character meaning.

Type B These relations connect characters that have in common their readings that are the Annamese ones (i.e., not derived from Chinese). The meanings of the Annamese words are identical or close to the original character meanings.

Type C These relations connect characters that have in common their readings that derive from the original Chinese

Phonetic relations   91

ones, but ignore the original character meanings. In other words, the meaning of the Annamese word corresponding to the reading is unrelated to the original character meaning.

Type D These relations connect Chữ nôm local characters that have in common their readings (and not necessarily their meanings). This relation could also be applied for characters originally introduced as Chữ nôm local characters, but that already existed in China (i.e., without being acknowledged at that time by the Chữ nôm script).

One should note that we are still dealing with phonetic relations here, not semantic ones. For instance, even though Type A relations connect two characters that each retains its original meaning, these two characters in relation with respect to the Type A relation do share the same reading (derived from Chinese) but do not necessarily share the same meaning. Examples for the Type A and Type D phonetic relations are given in Figure 4.6. As previously, we rely on valued edges to indicate the character reading that links two characters.

4.5.3 Japanese

Finally, we focus on the case of Japanese, which is by far the most complex. As recalled at the beginning of this section, Chinese character reading in Japanese particularly requires much

Character Relations

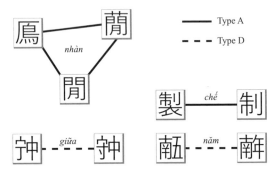

Figure 4.6: Illustrating the Type A and Type D phonetic relations between Chinese characters in Annamese.

attention as most characters have several different pronunciations. The various pronunciations as found in the Japanese language are detailed in Chapter 3. They are used here to define several phonetic relations between characters.

To illustrate the various phonetic relations between Chinese characters in Japanese, we define several types of edges to connect characters to each other, one type per pronunciation sort. Because the remarkable relations induced by the *kun* readings are discussed in detail in the next section, we define three edge types: one type for each of the three *go-on*, *kan-on*, and *tō-on* readings. We once again rely on valued edges to indicate the character reading that links two characters. Concrete examples of such phonetic relations are given in Figure 4.7.

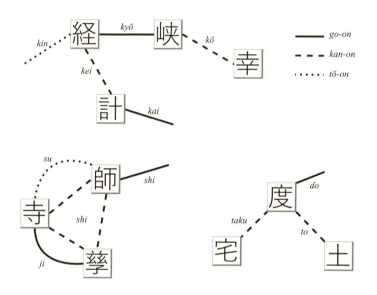

Figure 4.7: Illustrating the *on* phonetic relations between Chinese characters in Japanese.

Several topological properties can then be deduced.

Property 12. *The minimum degree in a graph induced by the kun and on (go-on, kan-on, and tō-on) phonetic relations is 1.*

94   *Character Relations*

Proof. As detailed in Chapter 3, every character in Japanese has at least one *kun* or *on* reading. Most characters have both, with the notable exception of *kokuji* characters that often only have *kun* readings. In the exceptional case that a character has a unique reading that is not shared by any other character, a loop edge (i.e., connecting the character to itself) is induced by the reflexivity property of phonetic relations.   □

Property 13. *The maximum degree in such a graph remains undefined.*

Effectively, a character can be incident with several edges of the same type (i.e., several different readings of the same sort, like two *kan-on* readings).

Finally, and as shown in Figure 4.7, such a graph can include double edges. This is the case when two characters share several reading sorts, for instance when they have the same *kan-on* and *go-on* readings.

4.6   Particular phonetic relations: *dōkun-iji*

To conclude this chapter on character relations, we focus in this section on a particular relational aspect of Chinese characters as found in Japanese. The kind of relation discussed henceforth still deals with character pronunciation and is therefore a continuation of Section 4.5.

Particular phonetic relations: dōkun-iji 95

Originally designed for the Chinese language, Chinese characters were subsequently exported to other regions of Asia. One issue thus being raised is that languages importing Chinese characters as writing system are not a perfect match between Chinese characters and the words found in the importing language. Effectively, some local words do not have a Chinese character equivalent (this is the issue of *kokuji*, discussed in Chapters 2 and 8), and, reciprocally, there may be no word in the importing language which matches a Chinese character, for instance, botanical species not found outside China – this is the issue of *dōkun-iji*.

"instruction,"
"reading"

Unsurprisingly, both issues are found within the Japanese language. We focus in this section on the latter, *dōkun-iji*. In its use of Chinese characters, the Japanese language features characters that have the same *kun* pronunciation (see Chapter 3) and that at the same time hold rather close meanings. Originally, this corresponds to the Chinese language providing a larger spectrum of semantic nuances than the importing language has. In other words, the importing language originally does not make the distinction the Chinese language does in some cases between rather close meanings.

For example (this is a made up example for clarity), where the Chinese language would have a character for "car," another one for "boat," and a third one for "plane," the importing language might only have one word "vehicle" to describe these

96   *Character Relations*

three characters. The granularity is simply different. This is indeed the previously described issue. That is, there is no word in the importing language (here Japanese) to match a Chinese character. Hence, the Japanese language assigns to several Chinese characters the same word (i.e., *kun* reading), yet retaining the semantic nuance induced by the Chinese characters.

We consider the Japanese verb *toru*, "to take." This word is assigned to several Chinese characters which are semantically close. For example (do not mind the *hiragana* る character on the right side of each Chinese character, whose sole purpose here is grammatical):

- 取る "to take" (general use)

- 撮る "to take [a picture]"

- 摂る "to take [medicine]"

- 盗る "to take [by stealing]"

These four Japanese verbs are all *toru*, "to take" but with semantic nuances.

Hence, it is possible to introduce a new character relation corresponding to this particular aspect of Japanese. We call this relation *dōkun*. The following property can be directly deduced from this definition.

Figure 4.8: Illustrating the *dōkun* relation: a complete graph is induced.

Property 14. *The dōkun relation is reflexive, symmetric, and transitive: for u, v, w any three characters, uRu, $uRv \Leftrightarrow vRu$, and $(uRv) \wedge (vRw) \Rightarrow uRw$ hold, with R the dōkun relation.*

From this property, interestingly and not encountered so far with the previously defined character relations, the *dōkun* relation induces sub-networks that are complete (in the sense of complete graph). A graph is complete if and only if each of its nodes is connected to every one of the other nodes in the graph. An illustration reusing the previous *toru*, "to take" example is given in Figure 4.8.

Furthermore, this graph completeness topological property remains satisfied whenever considering a variant (i.e., semantic relation, see Section 4.3) of characters related by the *dōkun* relation. Precisely, for a set $D = \{u_1, u_2, \ldots, u_n\}$ of characters

98   *Character Relations*

such that $u_i R u_j$ ($1 \leq i, j \leq n$, $i \neq j$) with R the *dōkun* relation, the graph induced by D with respect to R is a K_n (i.e., a complete graph of order n, a.k.a. *n*-complete). For u_i' a variant of u_i (i.e., $u_i' R' u_i$ with R' a semantic relation as of Section 4.3), the relation $u_i' R u_j$ ($1 \leq j \leq n, i \neq j$) holds and the graph induced by the set $D' = \{u_1, u_2, \ldots, u_{i-1}, u_i', u_{i+1}, \ldots, u_n\}$ with respect to R is also a K_n.

If a character variant is added to the network, that is, not in place of a character as previously but instead as a new network node, we have the following property: given u_i' a variant of u_i, say $u_i' R' u_i$ with R' a semantic relation, the graph induced by the set $D' = \{u_1, u_2, \ldots, u_{i-1}, u_i, u_i', u_{i+1}, \ldots, u_n\}$ is a K_{n+1} with respect to the two relations R and R'.

Figure 4.9 displays the case where the old form variant 攝 of the character 摂 is added to the network of Figure 4.8. Here, we have three remarkable different complete graphs: a K_4 induced by the set {取,撮,摂,盗} and another one by the set {取,撮,攝,盗}, both with respect to the *dōkun* relation, and a K_5 induced by the set {取,撮,摂,攝,盗} with respect to the *dōkun* and variant relations.

It is important to emphasize that on the one hand, asymmetric relations such as the form relations induce directed graphs (see Figure 4.3), and on the other hand, the phonetic relations such as the *dōkun* relation are symmetric (i.e., two-way) relations, in other words, that induce non-directed graphs (see Figure 4.9).

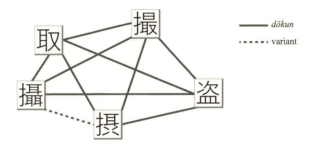

Figure 4.9: Illustrating the complete graphs induced by the *dōkun* and semantic relations (i.e., character variant).

Bibliographical notes

1. Graph notations, definitions, as well as numerous graph properties, including sub-graphs and complete graphs, are detailed, for instance, in the reference book "Graph theory" (fourth edition, Heidelberg, Germany: Springer, 2010) by Reinhard Diestel.

2. The Tang dynasty (618–907) dictionary *Ganlu zishu* (干禄字書, *Kanroku jisho* in Japanese), authored by Genson Gan from the 7th to the 8th century, gives an insightful overview of practical usage of early modern Chinese characters. This Chinese dictionary was created

100 *Character Relations*

as the official learning guide for the examination to become a public servant, mainly recording for 804 characters the orthodox form, acceptable form (i.e., character variants that have been in use for a long time and thus almost considered as correct forms), and vulgar form variants, for a grand total of 1,656 characters (refer for instance to the work "On relation types between orthodox and alternate character forms in *Ganlu zishu*" (『干禄字書』における正字・異体字関係の類型について, in Japanese) by Natsuki Fujita in Kokubun gakukō, 136:25–42, 1992). An 1880 edition in two volumes by the former Japanese publisher Ryūshindō (柳心堂) is available in the National Diet Library of Japan, including its online repository.

3. The Japanese characters that share one same pronunciation while expressing nuanced meanings (i.e., *dōkun-iji*) are reviewed in the very easy to read book "同訓異字辞典" by Hideko Asada (Tokyo, Japan: Tokyodo Shuppan (東京堂出版), 2012), and rigorously analyzed in the book "同訓異字" by Shizuka Shirakawa (Tokyo, Japan: Heibonsha (平凡社), 2014).

4. The character classification issue, including the categories defined by the six writings, is discussed, for instance, in the book "The origin and early development of the Chi-

Bibliographical notes   101

nese writing system" by William G. Boltz, (New Haven, CT, USA: American Oriental Society, 1993).

102   *Character Relations*

CHAPTER 5

Character Algebra: Going Beyond Relations

As presented in Chapter 4, Chinese characters include many variants for one single character, especially across languages and scripts, which adds to the complexity, and frankly, to the confusion. This issue actually reveals an important aspect of these characters: much evolution has been observed in time, even inside one same language or script. Typical examples include the character simplification reforms started by the Japanese and Chinese governments in 1946 and 1956, respectively

104   *Character Algebra: Going Beyond Relations*

(see Chapters 2 and 8). For various reasons, character identification is a challenging issue.

As briefly presented in Section 3.3, *sìjiǎo hàomǎ* (四角號碼, *shikaku gōma* in Japanese) is a well-known technique for Chinese character look-up. Effectively, due to their huge number, character look-up is a critical issue. *Sìjiǎo hàomǎ* relies on character elements to identify characters and realize a mapping between a character and its *sìjiǎo hàomǎ* code, which is made of four or five integers. However, this technique remains ambiguous because one single character can be mapped to several *sìjiǎo hàomǎ* codes, and one single code may induce the look-up of several characters. Here, we aim at proposing a character algebra, significantly reducing the ambiguity of *sìjiǎo hàomǎ* when realizing character decomposition. For completeness, we mention that a look-up system, SKIP,[1] similar to *sìjiǎo hàomǎ* but with even more indeterminism has also been described.

Precisely, our objective is to elegantly and meaningfully express the character systems that rely on Chinese characters. Elegantly in the sense that characters are described simply, algebraically, and unambiguously. Meaningfully in the sense that character decomposition and operations should reflect a character's historical origin and formation as much as possible. From another point of view, we aim at logically organizing such sets

---

[1]"The Kodansha kanji learner's dictionary," revised and expanded, New York, NY, USA: Kodansha USA, 2013.

Character Algebra: Going Beyond Relations   105

of Chinese characters.

Early steps of character decomposition (at that time aimed at automatic processing only) can be traced back to the work by Fujimura and Kagaya. Then, the work by Sproat considers further the theoretical aspect of such character decompositions by introducing the notion of planar regular languages and defining five decomposition operations for application to Chinese characters and Korean's Hangul. In this book, we further refine the theoretical aspect of Chinese characters.

Building on the proposed algebra, we describe, as application, a coding function for Chinese characters, in other words, a function mapping a distinct number to each character. This is a critical problem that is currently being researched under the sponsorship of the Chinese government. One essential point to be addressed is the coding of characters that are not covered by the Unicode standard. The work presented in this chapter describes a solution to this problem.

In addition, and importantly, this algebra work has profound educational virtues. Due to the huge number of characters involved, character memorization is an ongoing challenge, even for native speakers. By enabling the learner to rely on logical (algebraic) information, we provide additional content to support memorization. As discussed, for instance, by Yokoyama, there is an assured relation between character decomposition and Chinese character teaching. Indeed, relying on acquired knowledge has been proven to be critical support for educa-

106   *Character Algebra: Going Beyond Relations*

tion globally, as presented by Anderson in general with linking schema theory to education, and in particular for Chinese characters. This educational issue is even more critical for the special case of the Vietnamese Chữ nôm script, as the number of people being able to read and write this script is continuously decreasing. It has been estimated that only 100 people, most of them scholars, are still able to use the Chữ nôm script. As presented in Chapter 2, the Taberd dictionary is considered a reference work for Chữ nôm studies and it clearly illustrates the applicability of the method described here, namely characters' relations and decompositions.

In addition, one of the many interesting applications of this algebra is the expression of a character that is absent from the character set considered. For example, in the Japanese media, when mentioning a Chinese national by name, it is often the case that this person's name includes one or several characters that are absent from the Japanese character set in use in this media (usually the Japanese Industrial Standards Committee's standard JIS). Hence, as a last resort, the media will textually describe such a non-displayable character by giving the sub-characters composing it. This is a somewhat hazardous task which contains much ambiguity. This is so not only with persons' names but also recently with the case of Chinese vessels entering Japanese territorial waters: the Japanese media need to use the same tricks to mention vessels' names as employed characters are often not part of the JIS standard.

5.1 The universal character set $\mathbb{U}$

"collect,"
"group"

In this section, we formally discuss the different character sets considered in this chapter. Because it is too difficult to directly define the universal character set $\mathbb{U}$ that includes all Chinese characters, past and present, with their variants, we start by discussing the character sets currently in use in various languages. Subsequently, all these sets will enable the definition of the superset $\mathbb{U}$, including all the defined character sets, plus others.

First, we consider scripts separately (e.g., Chinese (traditional), Chinese (simplified), Japanese (*kanji*), Korean (*hanja*), Vietnamese (Chữ nôm), among others). We introduce three sets for each script: the real set, the radical set, and the support set, as defined below.

Definition 4. *Given a script, the* real set *for this script consists of all the characters that are currently in use in the corresponding language.*

Lemma 1. *A real set is a finite set.*

Proof. Given a language, a modern character dictionary for this language is an instance of the corresponding real set. In other words, a real set includes all the characters in use in the corresponding language at a fixed moment in time. □

108   *Character Algebra: Going Beyond Relations*

As an example of a real set, we define the set $\mathbb{J}$ that includes all the Chinese characters currently in use within the Japanese language. Concretely, we can consider that $\mathbb{J}$ is made of all the characters referenced in a standard Japanese characters dictionary (漢和辞典). We similarly define the real sets $\mathbb{C}_t$ and $\mathbb{C}_s$ for the characters used as of today in traditional and simplified Chinese, respectively.

We further specify real sets with the following definitions. We speak of character composition (or decomposition) here with respect to the decomposition operations introduced in the next section.

Definition 5. *A prime character is a character that cannot be further decomposed.*

Here, we clarify the difference between canonical and prime characters. On the one hand, a canonical character, as introduced in Chapter 4, is canonical with respect to the considered set of characters, that is, a restricted subset of Chinese characters as specified, for instance, for pedagogic applications. In other words, a canonical character cannot be decomposed with characters of the considered subset. On the other hand, a prime character is "absolutely canonical": it cannot be decomposed further with respect to the decomposition operations introduced in the next section. For example, considering the character set $\{杜, 地, 土, 也\}$, the character 杜 is canonical as it cannot be decomposed with characters of this set only, unlike the character

The universal character set $\mathbb{U}$ 109

地, which is a combination of the two characters 土 and 也, both included in the considered set. However, the character 杜 is not a prime character as it is the combination of the two characters 土 and 木.

Whether a character can be further decomposed or not remains to be discussed. This important issue is addressed in the rest of this section.

Definition 6. *For a real set R, the* radical set $\hat{R}$ *consists of the character radicals traditionally used for character look-up in dictionaries.*

As an example, the 214 conventional radicals of Table 3.6 correspond to the radical set for the Japanese *kanji* script, in other words, to the set $\hat{\mathbb{J}}$.

Next, we go on to the last character set: the support set. The meaning of this set may still be obscure after giving its definition. Nonetheless, it will emerge naturally after giving in Section 5.5 the inductive process we use to realize character decomposition. (We need to define first algebraic operations on character sets before describing such a process.) The objective of the support set is to facilitate character decomposition and keep such decomposition meaningful by fixing a "lower bound" preventing to over-decompose a character, that is, to reach a level where decompositions are no longer meaningful, for instance, as solely describing the connection of strokes together. Hence, the lower the number of elements inside the support set, the more

110   *Character Algebra: Going Beyond Relations*

general our character system description and thus the better the proposed decomposition methodology.

Definition 7. *For a real set R, the* support set *$\tilde{R}$ consists of the prime characters that are neither included in R nor $\hat{R}$ but that are decided by R to achieve character decomposition for the elements of R.*

As an example, we give in Table 5.1 elements of the set $\tilde{\mathbb{J}}$, in other words, the support set for the Japanese *kanji* script. It is worth noticing that an element of the support set could well be the composition of several elements, say, for instance, elements of the radical set. Nonetheless, as defined previously, the elements of the support set are always considered to be prime.

Remark 1. *Given a script (i.e., real set) R, we have by definition $\hat{R} \cap \tilde{R} = \emptyset$.*

Definition 8. *Given a script (i.e., real set) R, the set $\bar{R} = \hat{R} \cup \tilde{R}$ is the set of the prime characters for R.*

Even though we adapt it to our methodology, a similar task of prime element identification has been conducted in the past, see, for instance, the *sìjiǎo hàomǎ* character look-up method and the Wada fonts.

Remark 2. *Given two radical sets $\hat{S}$ and $\hat{T}$ corresponding to two different scripts (i.e., real sets) S and T, we have $|(\hat{S} \cup \hat{T}) \setminus (\hat{S} \cap \hat{T})| \approx 0$.*

The universal character set $\mathbb{U}$ 111

Table 5.1: Examples of elements of the support set $\tilde{\mathbb{J}}$: elements not in $\mathbb{J} \cup \hat{\mathbb{J}}$ but decided by $\mathbb{J}$.

In $\tilde{\mathbb{J}}$	Induced by	In $\tilde{\mathbb{J}}$	Induced by
冋	同	𦥯	覺, 學, etc.
川	弗, 井, etc.	𣴎	無, 舞, etc.
屮	亞	中	亜
䒑	学, 觉, etc.	靣	画
夕	卯	𠕁	令
俊	夜	力	万
辵	卸	鱼	強
匚	印	彐	今
奚	鶏, 渓, etc.	开	形, 研, etc.
僉	険, 験, etc.	雚	勧, 権, etc.

For instance, considering the real set for traditional Chinese $\mathbb{C}_t$, we have $\hat{\mathbb{C}}_t = \hat{\mathbb{J}}$. Considering the real set for simplified Chinese $\mathbb{C}_s$, we have $\hat{\mathbb{C}}_s = (\hat{\mathbb{J}} \setminus \{龍\}) \cup \{户, 见, 讠, 贝, 车, 钅, 长, 门, 韦, 页, 风, 飞, 饣, 马, 鱼, 鸟, 齐, 齿, 龙, 龟\}$. Even more precisely, these additional radicals with respect to the real set $\mathbb{C}_s$ should simply be considered radical variants, as mentioned previously, and thus, we would simply have $\hat{\mathbb{C}}_s = \hat{\mathbb{J}} \setminus \{龍\}$.

In addition, we have the following lemmas.

112   *Character Algebra: Going Beyond Relations*

Lemma 2. *For a real set R, the two sets R and $\hat{R}$ are not necessarily disjoint.*

Proof. The character 一 is inside $\mathbb{J} \cap \hat{\mathbb{J}}$.   □

Lemma 3. *For a real set R, the sets $\hat{R}$ and $\tilde{R}$ are both finite.*

Proof. Obviously, since any real set R is finite, the corresponding sets $\hat{R}$ and $\tilde{R}$ are finite.   □

From this discussion, we can define the universal set of prime characters $\bar{\mathbb{U}}$.

Definition 9. *For a finite set $\mathscr{R}$ of real sets, we have*

$$\bar{\mathbb{U}} = \bigcup_{R \in \mathscr{R}} \hat{R} \cup \tilde{R}$$

Lemma 4. *The set $\bar{\mathbb{U}}$ is finite.*

Proof. By Definition 9 and Lemma 3, $\bar{\mathbb{U}}$ is a finite union of finite sets. Hence, $\bar{\mathbb{U}}$ is finite.   □

From this discussion, we can now deduce the universal set $\mathbb{U}$ that consists of all the Chinese characters. The set $\mathbb{U}$ is defined as follows.

Definition 10. *The set $\mathbb{U}$ consists of*

- *prime characters (i.e., elements of $\bar{\mathbb{U}}$);*

The universal character set $\mathbb{U}$ 113

- *algebraic combinations of any two (or three) elements of* $\mathbb{U}$.

We obviously have $\bar{\mathbb{U}} \subset \mathbb{U}$. Because $\mathbb{U}$ also includes all the characters that result from the combination of any two elements of $\mathbb{U}$, we have the following lemma.

Lemma 5. *The universal set* $\mathbb{U}$ *is not finite.*

Proof. Assume $\mathbb{U} = \{u_1, u_2, \ldots, u_k\}$ is a finite character set. Assume without loss of generality that $u_i \leq u_{i+1}$ ($1 \leq i < k$) with $\leq$ being the order relation between any two characters with respect to their numbers of strokes. In $\mathbb{U}$, the character u_k has thus the highest number of strokes. Hence, for any character $u_i \in \mathbb{U}$, and for any character combination (binary) operation $\bullet$ on $\mathbb{U}$ as defined in Section 5.2, the character $u_i \bullet u_k$ obviously has more strokes than the character u_k and is thus not in $\mathbb{U}$, which is a contradiction (as per Definition 10). Therefore, $\mathbb{U}$ is of infinite cardinality. $\qquad\square$

For instance, considering only the Chinese and Japanese character sets, $\mathbb{U}$ can be recursively defined as follows.

$$\mathbb{U} = \left(\mathbb{C}_s \cup \hat{\mathbb{C}}_s \cup \tilde{\mathbb{C}}_s\right) \cup \left(\mathbb{C}_t \cup \hat{\mathbb{C}}_t \cup \tilde{\mathbb{C}}_t\right) \cup \left(\mathbb{J} \cup \hat{\mathbb{J}} \cup \tilde{\mathbb{J}}\right)$$
$$\cup \{u_1 \bullet u_2 \mid \forall u_1, u_2 \in \mathbb{U}\}$$

The set $\mathbb{U}$ is indeed not finite. For the sake of clarity, the operation $\bullet$ stands for any binary character combination operation as

114   *Character Algebra: Going Beyond Relations*

defined in Section 5.2. Ternary combination operations can be similarly included in the definition of $\mathbb{U}$.

Finally, we define the following relations for the elements of $\mathbb{U}$.

Definition 11. *For two elements $u, v \in \mathbb{U}$, the equality relation $u = v$ holds if and only if u is the same element as v.*

And obviously,

Property 15. *The equality relation on $\mathbb{U}$ is reflexive, symmetric, and transitive.*

Conversely,

Definition 12. *For two elements $u, v \in \mathbb{U}$, the inequality relation $u \neq v$ holds if and only if u and v are distinct.*

And obviously,

Property 16. *The inequality relation on $\mathbb{U}$ is symmetric.*

5.2 Composition operations

We describe in this section the algebraic operations on the universal set $\mathbb{U}$.

Although in $\mathbb{J}$ only, we first introduced in a preliminary work three character composition operations $(+, \times, \text{and} -)$. Describing the complete real set $\mathbb{J}$ of the Chinese characters used

Composition operations 115

in the Japanese writing system with only these three operations has proven very difficult, and with a certain degree of ambiguity possibly remaining for character expressions. So, aiming to further eliminate such ambiguity and to include the other scripts, we expand here on this previous work by introducing seventeen different character composition operations. One can note that the symbols for some of these operations can be found in the Unicode "Ideographic Description Characters" range (2FF0–2FFF). These few Unicode symbols do not aim at completely describing character decompositions though. In addition, similar patterns have been previously distinguished but for character radicals only (偏旁冠脚) in the *Kadokawa saishin kanwa jiten* dictionary.[2]

"tie," "join"

To simplify our notations, we first describe semantically and name the seventeen character composition operations on $\mathbb{U}$ (see Table 5.2). In this table, each entry of the "Symbol" column describes the arrangement of sub-characters for the corresponding operation. Formal operation definitions are given subsequently.

The identity operation ϕ_0 is mostly for the purpose of classification, as when, for example, referencing and counting the character decomposition operations that are in use for a particular character set. In such case, the ϕ_0 operation may be selected,

---

[2] 角川 最新漢和辞典, Tokyo, Japan: Kadokawa (角川), 1995.

116   *Character Algebra: Going Beyond Relations*

Table 5.2: The character composition operations in $\mathbb{U}$.

Operation	Symbol	Description
ϕ_0		identity
ϕ_1		horizontal combination
ϕ_2		vertical combination
ϕ_3		surrounding combination
ϕ_4		left-bottom combination
ϕ_5		top-right combination
ϕ_6		left-top combination
ϕ_7		n-shape combination
ϕ_8		C-shape combination
ϕ_9		U-shape combination
ϕ_{10}		M-shape combination
ϕ_{11}		W-shape combination
ϕ_{12}		T-shape combination
ϕ_{13}		reversed T combination
ϕ_{14}		horizontal split (stretch)
ϕ_{15}		vertical split (stretch)
ϕ_{16}		superposition combination

Composition operations   117

for instance, when encountering elements that are in the radical set.

The superposition operation ϕ_{16} may be tempting for many characters. However, to retain the origin and essence of a character, other operations are, most of the time, more suitable. For example, it might be considered that the character 囚 could be decomposed as the superposition of 囗 and 人. Yet, it is more suitable (i.e., meaningful) to decompose this character with the surrounding operation ϕ_3 instead. In fact, the character 囗 is the radical whose meaning includes that of "surrounding," and with 人 "man," the meaning of 囚 "prisoner" is naturally induced. The superposition operation usage must be limited to the character decompositions for which it makes sense to superpose elements, e.g., 中 decomposed as the superposition of 囗 and 丨 (in fact, the superposition operation naturally suits well the characters of the ideogram category (see Section 3.2) that use an element to indicate a specific part of another element, such as the character 中 and, for instance, the character 本 as explained in Chapter 3). Usually, the superposition operation would be used when no other operation is suitable.

As mentioned, the identity operation ϕ_0 is mostly used for classification. Each of the other operations is formally defined hereinafter. For more clarity, an example will be given for each operation. First, we define the operations ϕ_1 to ϕ_9.

118   *Character Algebra: Going Beyond Relations*

Definition 13.   **Definition 14.**

E.g. In $\mathbb{J}$, and thus in $\mathbb{U}$, considering the three characters 木,南,楠 $\in \mathbb{J}$ ("tree," "south," and "camphor tree," respectively), we have 楠 $=$ 木ϕ_1南.

E.g. In $\mathbb{J}$, and thus in $\mathbb{U}$, considering the three characters 山,石,岩 $\in \mathbb{J}$ ("mountain," "stone," and "rock," respectively), we have 岩 $=$ 山ϕ_2石.

Definition 15.   **Definition 16.**

E.g. In $\mathbb{J}$, and thus in $\mathbb{U}$, considering the three characters 国,囗,玉 $\in \mathbb{J}$, we have 国 $=$ 囗ϕ_3玉.

E.g. In $\mathbb{U}$, for the radical 辶 $\in \hat{\mathbb{J}}$ and the two characters 首,道 $\in \mathbb{J}$, we have 道 $=$ 辶ϕ_4首.

Definition 17.

$$\phi_5 \; : \; \mathbb{U} \times \mathbb{U} \; \rightarrow \; \mathbb{U}$$

$$u \, \phi_5 \, v \; \mapsto \; \boxed{\begin{array}{c} ^{v} \\ u \end{array}}$$

Definition 18.

$$\phi_6 \; : \; \mathbb{U} \times \mathbb{U} \; \rightarrow \; \mathbb{U}$$

$$u \, \phi_6 \, v \; \mapsto \; \boxed{\begin{array}{c} u \\ v \end{array}}$$

E.g. In $\mathbb{U}$, for the radical 勹 $\in \hat{\mathbb{J}}$ and the two characters 日, 旬 $\in \mathbb{J}$, we have 旬 $=$ 日 ϕ_5 勹.

E.g. In $\mathbb{U}$, for the radical 厂 $\in \hat{\mathbb{J}}$ and the two characters 泉, 原 $\in \mathbb{J}$, we have 原 $=$ 厂 ϕ_6 泉.

Definition 19.

$$\phi_7 \; : \; \mathbb{U} \times \mathbb{U} \; \rightarrow \; \mathbb{U}$$

$$u \, \phi_7 \, v \; \mapsto \; \boxed{\begin{array}{c} u \\ v \end{array}}$$

Definition 20.

$$\phi_8 \; : \; \mathbb{U} \times \mathbb{U} \; \rightarrow \; \mathbb{U}$$

$$u \, \phi_8 \, v \; \mapsto \; \boxed{u \, | \, v}$$

E.g. In $\mathbb{J}$, and thus in $\mathbb{U}$, considering the three characters 門, 各, 閣 $\in \mathbb{J}$, we have 閣 $=$ 門 ϕ_7 各.

E.g. In $\mathbb{U}$, for the radical 匚 $\in \hat{\mathbb{J}}$ and the two characters 矢, 医 $\in \mathbb{J}$, we have 医 $=$ 匚 ϕ_8 矢.

120   *Character Algebra: Going Beyond Relations*

Definition 21.

$$\phi_9 \; : \; \mathbb{U} \times \mathbb{U} \; \to \; \mathbb{U}$$

$$u \; \phi_9 \; v \; \mapsto \; \boxed{\begin{array}{c} u \\ \hline v \end{array}}$$

E.g. In $\mathbb{U}$, for the radical $\sqcup \in \hat{\mathbb{J}}$ and the two characters $\nearrow, \boxtimes \in \mathbb{J}$, we have $\boxtimes = \nearrow \phi_9 \sqcup$.

We define the operations ϕ_{10} to ϕ_{16} below. For the operations ϕ_{10} to ϕ_{12}, no character is known to the author such that ternary, rather than binary, operations are needed. For instance, the character 繭 might seem to require ϕ_{10} to be a ternary operation; however, the element below ⁺⁺ is actually not in the real set $\mathbb{J}$ but in the support set $\tilde{\mathbb{J}}$. Yet, as there might actually exist a character requiring a ternary operation definition, we precautiously define ϕ_{10} to ϕ_{12} as ternary operations. Regarding ϕ_{13}, the only actual character known to the author that requires a ternary operation definition is the character 坐, which is a variant of the character 坐. Hence, the definitions of ϕ_{10} to ϕ_{13} include a ternary operator ϕ_j^i with $i = 1, 2$ and $j = 10, 11, 12, 13$. For the two character-splitting operations ϕ_{14} and ϕ_{15}, by definition they are binary operations – the split (stretch) leaving space for one additional element – and not ternary.

Composition operations 121

Definition 22.

$$\phi_{10} \ : \ \mathbb{U} \times \mathbb{U} \times \mathbb{U} \ \rightarrow \ \mathbb{U}$$

$$u \ \phi_{10}^1 \ v \ \phi_{10}^2 \ w \ \mapsto \ \boxed{\begin{array}{c} u \\ \hline v \ w \end{array}}$$

Definition 23.

$$\phi_{11} \ : \ \mathbb{U} \times \mathbb{U} \times \mathbb{U} \ \rightarrow \ \mathbb{U}$$

$$u \ \phi_{11}^1 \ v \ \phi_{11}^2 \ w \ \mapsto \ \boxed{\begin{array}{c} v \ w \\ \hline u \end{array}}$$

E.g. In $\mathbb{J}$, and thus in $\mathbb{U}$, considering the three characters 帀, 入, 兩 $\in \mathbb{J}$, we have 兩 $=$ 帀 ϕ_{10}^1 入 ϕ_{10}^2 入.

E.g. In $\mathbb{U}$, for the radical 幺 $\in \hat{\mathbb{J}}$ and the two characters 山, 幽 $\in \mathbb{J}$, we have 幽 $=$ 山 ϕ_{11}^1 幺 ϕ_{11}^2 幺.

Definition 24.

$$\phi_{12} \ : \ \mathbb{U} \times \mathbb{U} \times \mathbb{U} \ \rightarrow \ \mathbb{U}$$

$$u \ \phi_{12}^1 \ v \ \phi_{12}^2 \ w \ \mapsto \ \boxed{\begin{array}{c} u \\ \hline v \ w \end{array}}$$

Definition 25.

$$\phi_{13} \ : \ \mathbb{U} \times \mathbb{U} \times \mathbb{U} \ \rightarrow \ \mathbb{U}$$

$$u \ \phi_{13}^1 \ v \ \phi_{13}^2 \ w \ \mapsto \ \boxed{\begin{array}{c} v \ w \\ \hline u \end{array}}$$

E.g. In $\mathbb{U}$, for the two radicals 羊, 言 $\in \hat{\mathbb{J}}$, we have 譱 $=$ 羊 ϕ_{12}^1 言 ϕ_{12}^2 言.

E.g. In $\mathbb{J}$, and thus in $\mathbb{U}$, considering the four characters 土, 口, 人, 坐 $\in \mathbb{J}$, we have 坐 $=$ 土 ϕ_{13}^1 口 ϕ_{13}^2 人.

122 *Character Algebra: Going Beyond Relations*

Definition 26.

$$\phi_{14} \; : \; \mathbb{U} \times \mathbb{U} \; \to \; \mathbb{U}$$

$$u \; \phi_{14} \; v \; \mapsto \; \boxed{u\,v\,u}$$

(u is split (stretched).)

Definition 27.

$$\phi_{15} \; : \; \mathbb{U} \times \mathbb{U} \; \to \; \mathbb{U}$$

$$u \; \phi_{15} \; v \; \mapsto \; \boxed{\begin{array}{c} u \\ v \\ u \end{array}}$$

(u is split (stretched).)

E.g. In $\mathbb{J}$, and thus in $\mathbb{U}$, considering the three characters 街, 圭, 行 $\in \mathbb{J}$, we have 街 $=$ 行 ϕ_{14} 圭.

E.g. In $\mathbb{J}$, and thus in $\mathbb{U}$, considering the three characters 吏, 丈, 口 $\in \mathbb{J}$, we have 吏 $=$ 丈 ϕ_{15} 口.

Definition 28.

$$\phi_{16} \; : \; \mathbb{U} \times \mathbb{U} \; \to \; \mathbb{U}$$

$$u \; \phi_{16} \; v \; \mapsto \; \boxed{\begin{array}{c} u \\ v \end{array}}$$

E.g. In $\mathbb{U}$, for the radical 丶 $\in \hat{\mathbb{J}}$ and the two characters 丼, 井 $\in \mathbb{J}$, we have 丼 $=$ 井 ϕ_{16} 丶.

We now state two important properties for these character composition operations in $\mathbb{U}$.

Property 17. *The operations ϕ_i ($0 \leq i \leq 16$) are non-associative and non-commutative.*

Composition operations   123

The non-commutativity property is obvious. Operation associativity is detailed in Sections 5.3 and 5.4.

Property 18. *The operations ϕ_i ($0 \leq i \leq 16$) have the same priority.*

In the rest of this book, for the sake of clarity, we often use the aliases $+$ and $\times$ for the two operations ϕ_1 and ϕ_2, respectively, and more generally, an operation ϕ_i is sometimes referred to simply as its index i, called the operation ID. In addition, as a character is usually composed of several others, we distinguish the topmost decomposition operation as the operation that should first be considered for correct and meaningful character decomposition. For instance, for the character 浜, which can be decomposed as 氵 $+$ (丘 $\times$ 八), the topmost operation is $+$. In other words, this is the operation at the top of the expression evaluation tree. Focusing on the topmost decomposition operations is indeed meaningful as we follow a recursive approach to character decomposition, as detailed in Section 5.5.

We conclude this section by giving additional properties and notations for the elements of the set $\mathbb{U}$. Considering the two operations $+$ and $\times$ (i.e., ϕ_1 and ϕ_2, respectively), that is, the operations that cover the vast majority of Chinese characters as shown in Section 5.6, factors and exponents can be naturally defined as follows.

Definition 29. *Given a natural number $k \in \mathbb{N}^*$ and an element*

124   *Character Algebra: Going Beyond Relations*

$u \in \mathbb{U}$, *the factor operation is defined from* $\mathbb{N}^* \times \mathbb{U}$ *into* $\mathbb{U}$ *as:*

$$ku = \underbrace{u + u + \ldots + u}_{k \text{ terms}}$$

E.g. The equality relation 琳 $=$ 王 $+$ 林 $=$ 王 $+ 2$木 holds.

Definition 30. *Given a natural number* $k \in \mathbb{N}^*$ *and an element* $u \in \mathbb{U}$, *the exponent operation is defined from* $\mathbb{N}^* \times \mathbb{U}$ *into* $\mathbb{U}$ *as:*

$$u^k = \underbrace{u \times u \times \ldots \times u}_{k \text{ factors}}$$

E.g. The equality relation 昌 $=$ 日 $\times$ 日 $=$ 日^2 holds.

It is important to note that 0 has been excluded on purpose from the possible factor and exponent values (i.e., the range of k). Effectively, given an element $u \in \mathbb{U}$, the factor operation $0u$ is undefined: 0 would be the expected result but $0 \notin \mathbb{U}$. Similarly for the exponent operation, given an element $u \in \mathbb{U}$, the exponent operation u^0 is undefined: 1 would be the expected result but $1 \notin \mathbb{U}$.

Next, it is critical to precisely describe the priority order of the factor and exponent operations in $\mathbb{U}$.

Property 19. *In* $\mathbb{U}$, *the factor and exponent operations have the same priority, and it is higher than those of the operations* ϕ_i *(*$0 \leq i \leq 16$*).*

Composition operations   125

E.g. For the two characters 森, 木 $\in \mathbb{J}$, the relations 森 $=$ 木 $\times$ (木 $+$ 木) $=$ 木 $\times$ 2木 and 木 $\times$ 2木 $\neq$ 2木^2 hold.

This is indeed a significant difference with regard to algebra on real numbers. This difference can be explained by the fact that in $\mathbb{U}$, we have 2木 $\neq$ 2 $\times$ 木 since the domain of the operation $\times$ is not $\mathbb{N} \times \mathbb{U}$ but $\mathbb{U} \times \mathbb{U}$.

Finally, in the case the meaning of the character decomposition does not matter, the following two properties can be added to the character algebra for the sake of completeness.

Property 20. *Both distributivity and factorization are applicable to the factor and exponent operations.*

E.g. Assuming the meaning of the character decomposition does not matter, the relations 競 $=$ 2(立 $\times$ 口 $\times$ 儿) $=$ 2立 $\times$ 2口 $\times$ 2儿 and 叕 $=$ 双^2 $=$ (又 $+$ 又)^2 $=$ 又^2 $+$ 又^2 each illustrate both distributivity (reading the equality from left to right) and factorization (reading the equality from right to left).

But again, since distributivity and factorization change the meaning of the decomposition, these two algebraic properties are not used often in practice. In the rest of this book, unless stated otherwise, characters are decomposed meaningfully.

As discussed in detail in Section 4.3, Chinese characters frequently have variants. To reflect this property in the proposed algebra, we conveniently rely on the congruence (equivalence) relation.

126   *Character Algebra: Going Beyond Relations*

Definition 31. *For two elements* $u, v \in \mathbb{U}$, *the relation* $u \equiv v$ *holds if and only if u is a variant of v.*

And obviously,

Property 21. *The congruence relation on* $\mathbb{U}$ *is reflexive, symmetric, and transitive.*

E.g. The character 島 "island" has several variants, including 嶋, 嶌, and 嶹. Hence, the equivalence relation 島 ≡ 嶋 = 山 + 鳥 ≡ 嶌 = 山 × 鳥 holds.

Furthermore, the congruence relation on $\mathbb{U}$ may induce identity between the two operations $+$ and $\times$.

E.g. The relation 嶋 ≡ 嶌 induces the relation 山 + 鳥 ≡ 山 × 鳥.

Moreover, the congruence relation on $\mathbb{U}$ may, in some rare cases, induce commutativity between the two operations $+$ and $\times$.

E.g. The relation 島 ≡ 嶌 ≡ 嶹 induces the relation 山 × 鳥 ≡ 鳥 × 山.

5.3   Character connectivity

We now enhance the previously described operations to consider left associativity and right associativity. The motivation behind this is as follows. Considering an algebraic expression on $\mathbb{U}$, the evaluation of this expression to form the corresponding character of $\mathbb{U}$ may occur differently since by Property 18, several operations of $\mathbb{U}$ have the same priority. Conventionally, in the absence of parentheses, operations of the same priority would be evaluated from left to right, but this is not a necessity. This may actually lead to a non-natural character decomposition, that is nonetheless algebraically correct.

"connection,"
"link"

For instance, let us consider the character 琳 $\in$ $\mathbb{J}$. This character can be decomposed in $\mathbb{U}$ as 琳 $=$ 王 $+$ 木 $+$ 木. Because not including parentheses, this expression could be evaluated either in the order 王 $+$ (木 $+$ 木) or, erroneously, in the order (王 $+$ 木) $+$ 木. Yet, the second evaluation order, meaning evaluating first the operation 王 $+$ 木, cannot be done in $\mathbb{J}$ as the character resulting from 王 $+$ 木 is not in $\mathbb{J}$ (it is indeed not a Japanese character). Nonetheless, this operation is legal in $\mathbb{U}$. More generally, this example shows that composition operations are not associative, and this for the same reason that distributivity and factorization are rarely used: the order in which operations are evaluated is significant with respect to the meaning of the character decomposition.

While in the particular case of 琳 above parentheses would suffice to remove evaluation order ambiguity, it is nevertheless interesting and useful to address this issue by refining the composition operations as follows.

Definition 32. *In $\mathbb{U}$, the operations $\overleftarrow{\phi_i}$ and $\overrightarrow{\phi_i}$ realize the left-*

128   *Character Algebra: Going Beyond Relations*

associative ϕ_i operation and the right-associative ϕ_i operation, respectively (1 $\leq i \leq$ 16).

Importantly, to mix the conventional ϕ_i with the left- and right-associative operations of Definition 32 in a single algebraic expression, we state the following property.

Property 22. *The left- and right-associative operations $\overleftarrow{\phi_i}$ and $\overrightarrow{\phi_i}$ have a higher priority than the regular ϕ_i operation (1 $\leq i \leq$ 16).*

Hence, to realize the decomposition of a character of a real set into that same real set, we may have to use the left-associative and right-associative operations defined previously. For example, considering once again the decomposition 琳 $=$ 王 $+$ 木 $+$ 木, we use the right-associative operation $\overrightarrow{+}$ and we have 王 $+$ 木$\overrightarrow{+}$木 $=$ 王 $+$ 林 $=$ 琳. Note that 王 $+$ 木$\overrightarrow{+}$木 $=$ 王$\overrightarrow{+}$木$\overrightarrow{+}$木 because of Property 22. Therefore, to decompose in $\mathbb{J}$ the character 琳 using exclusively the two characters 王 and 木, we must use the right-associative operation $\overrightarrow{+}$, as shown above.

When conducting automatic processing, these enhanced associativity considerations will play a critical role by providing information on the connectivity of the multiple characters being used to form another one. For instance, in the case of font generation and character graphical rendering, such information is essential for the distribution of space between the several elements making up a character.

5.4 Stroke order and connectivity

"order," "sequence"

Another important aspect of Chinese characters is the order in which they are written. Because overwhelmingly covering regular-use characters, we focus in this section on the two operations $+$ and $\times$ for clarity. One should note that this discussion could be reasonably extended to most of the other operations defined previously in Section 5.2, with a few unavoidable exceptions though, like ϕ_3. As mentioned in Section 3.1, the writing order of a character follows in general a top-to-bottom and left-to-right order. This is reflected by the following properties.

Property 23. *The operation $+$ reflects the writing order: $a+b$ induces that a is written before b, with a few exceptions, such as when b includes* 戈 *(e.g.,* 成, 識, *yet not* 戦*).*

Property 24. *The operation $\times$ reflects the writing order: $a \times b$ induces that a is written before b, with a few exceptions, such as for* 由 *(meaningfully decomposed as* ｜ $\times$ 田*).*

Such information induced by the writing order is yet another characteristic that one should consider when formally describ-

130   *Character Algebra: Going Beyond Relations*

ing this writing system. In fact, we will show in this section using algebraic expressions that the writing order of a character is directly related to the connectivity of its sub-characters. Such connectivity is expressed naturally with left- and right-associative operations.

Property 25. *With a few exceptions just as in Properties 23 and 24, the evaluation order of left-associative operations follows the character writing order, and the evaluation order of right-associative operations follows the reverse character writing order.*

Property 25 is explained below with supporting examples.

First, we discuss the case of left-associative operations. Consider without loss of generality the character 準 and its decomposition 氵十隹×十. First, since using left-associative operations, 氵 is first "evaluated" and returned as is. Then, the operation 氵十隹 is evaluated, inducing the character 淮. Lastly, 淮×十 is evaluated, inducing the character 準. This evaluation order reflects the connectivity of the sub-characters that form the character 準. We may also observe that this is the same order as the writing order: the character 準 is indeed written in the order 氵 → 隹 → 十.

Second, we discuss the case of right-associative operations. Consider without loss of generality the character 湘 and its possible decomposition 氵十木十目. Since using right-associative operations, 目 is first "evaluated" and returned as is. Then, the operation 木$\overrightarrow{+}$目 is evaluated, inducing the character 相. Lastly, 氵$\overrightarrow{+}$相 is evaluated, inducing the character 湘. This evaluation order reflects the connectivity of the sub-characters that form the character 湘. We may also observe that this is the reverse writing order: the character 湘 is indeed written in the order 氵 → 木 → 目.

Finally, both left- and right-associative operations can be mixed inside the same algebraic expression. Consider without loss of generality the character 箱 and its possible decomposition 箱 = ケ$\overleftarrow{+}$ケ × 木$\overrightarrow{+}$目. First, since by Property 22 the operation × has a lower priority than both $\overleftarrow{+}$ and $\overrightarrow{+}$, ケ is first "evaluated" and returned as is. Then, the operation ケ$\overleftarrow{+}$ケ is evaluated, inducing the character 竹 and reflecting the writing order. Next, the operation 木$\overrightarrow{+}$目 is evaluated, inducing first the character 目 as is. Then, 相 is obtained, reflecting the reverse writing order. And, by Property 24, the × operation does not affect the writing order. This concludes the discussion of Property 25.

Remark 3. *In the case of one single left- or right-associative operation, both operations can be identically used. Thus, even though character decomposition follows the writing order as by Property 25, this decomposition is not unique. For example, we have* 相 = 木$\overrightarrow{+}$目 = 木$\overleftarrow{+}$目.

Following this remark, one could imagine that in such cases of one single left- or right-associative operation, we simply use the conventional operation + or ×, and we obtain, this time, a unique decomposition. However, this does not hold in the case where several such single associative operations are used separately. For instance, the relation 箱 = ケ$\overset{\leftarrow}{+}$ケ × 木$\overset{\rightarrow}{+}$目 holds (left- and right-associative operations can be used indistinctly as mentioned previously in Remark 3), yet we have 箱 ≠ ケ + ケ × 木 + 目.

5.5   Automatic processing

"movement," "action"

We first describe, in Algorithm 1, the recursive process that can be used to automatically decompose and process a character as presented earlier in this chapter. Here, prime characters are considered terminal, while others are used to apply the decomposition algorithm recursively. This is the actual algorithm we use in this chapter to algebraically express a character function of others.

We then give, in Algorithm 2, an example of how to automatically process an algebraic expression in $\mathbb{U}$, respecting the evaluation order imposed by operations (namely, left associativity, right associativity, or unspecified associativity). Note that for the sake of clarity, this sample algorithm has been described for binary operations only.

From a statistical point of view 133

Algorithm 1: DECOMPOSE(c)

Input: One character $c \in \mathbb{U}$.

case $c \in \hat{\mathbb{U}}$ **do** // c in the radical set
  | Process c; // e.g., print
  | break;

case $c \in \tilde{\mathbb{U}}$ **do** // c in the support set
  | Process c; // e.g., print
  | break;

otherwise do // c in the real set and not in the radical set
  | Identify the topmost decomposition operation op;
  | Let $e_1, e_2, \ldots, e_n$ be the operands of op, with n the arity of op;
  | **for** $i = 1$ **to** n **do**
  | | DECOMPOSE(e_i);
  | **end**
end

5.6 From a statistical point of view

In this section, we give quantitative information regarding character decomposition operations. First, we focus on the regular-use Chinese characters in Japanese. We then analyze a pedagogical material used to teach Chinese characters to foreign learners.

134   *Character Algebra: Going Beyond Relations*

Algorithm 2: EVAL($e_1 o_1 e_2 o_2 \ldots o_{n-1} e_n$)

Input: An algebraic expression for a character $c \in \mathbb{U}$ with
$c = e_1 o_1 e_2 o_2 \ldots o_{n-1} e_n$ where $e_i \in \mathbb{U}$ ($1 \leq i \leq n$) and o_j
($1 \leq j \leq n-1$) one of the binary operations in $\mathbb{U}$.

Output: The character corresponding to the evaluation result of the
algebraic expression given as input.

Procedure COMBINE(e_1, op, e_2)

| c = combine e_1 and e_2 according to the operation op;
| **return** c

end

Procedure SIMPLE-EVAL($e_1 o_1 e_2 o_2 \ldots o_{n-1} e_n$)

| // Here, all the operations o_i ($1 \leq i \leq n-1$) have the same
| associativity (i.e., left, right, or unspecified).
| **case** o_1 right-associative **do**
| | x = COMBINE(e_{n-1}, o_{n-1}, e_n);
| | **return** SIMPLE-EVAL($e_1 o_1 e_2 o_2 \ldots o_{n-2} x$)
| **case** o_1 left-associative or non-associative **do**
| | x = COMBINE(e_1, o_1, e_2);
| | **return** SIMPLE-EVAL($x o_2 e_3 \ldots e_n$)

end

Array *parts*[], *ops*[]; $i = 0$;

while c not null **do**

| (*part*, *op*, c) = split c into *part*, *op*, and c at the first unspecified
| associativity operation *op*;
| *parts*[i] = SIMPLE-EVAL(*part*); *ops*[i] = *op*; $i = i + 1$;

$c = parts[0]\, ops[0]\, parts[1] \ldots ops[i-2]\, parts[i-1]$; // The final
expression (exclusively unspecified associativity operations).

return SIMPLE-EVAL(c)

5.6.1 Regular-use Chinese characters in Japanese

It is obviously important to confirm the following.

Remark 4. *The fifteen operations $\{\phi_i \mid 0 \leq i \leq 16, i \neq 10, 12\}$ cover the topmost decomposition operations of all the 2,136 regular-use Chinese characters in Japanese (*常用漢字*).*

"number,"
"count"

As proof, the topmost decomposition operations for all the 2,136 regular-use Chinese characters in Japanese are given in Tables A.1 and A.2 in appendix. The topmost operation repartition is given in Figure 5.1. It is worth noting that this repartition matches that obtained from a similar study (radical placement) conducted on characters of traditional Chinese as per the Big5 encoding standard by Jason Wang.[3]

5.6.2 Teaching material for foreign students

In this section, we consider a subset of the Chinese characters used in Japanese as taught at the Tokyo University of Agriculture and Technology (TUAT) as of October 2014 for the Japanese language class given to foreign students originating from

---
[3]"Toward a generative grammar of Chinese character structure and stroke order," Ph.D. thesis, University of Wisconsin, Madison, WI, USA, 1983.

136   *Character Algebra: Going Beyond Relations*

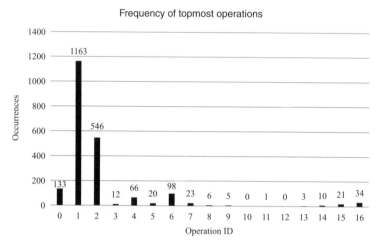

Figure 5.1: Repartition of the topmost decomposition operations for the regular-use Chinese characters in Japanese (常用漢字).

countries whose writing systems do not rely on Chinese characters. The main objectives of this course include enabling the recognition of Chinese character shapes, meanings, pronunciations, and writing in general. This course mostly relies on one material, the *"Basic kanji book"* by Chieko Kano, Yuri Shimizu, Hiroko Takenaka, and Eriko Ishii,[4] which includes the characters listed in Tables 5.3 and 5.4. Considering the set $\bar{\mathbb{J}}$ of the prime characters for the Japanese language, we summarize the

---

[4]Tokyo, Japan: Bonjinsha (凡人社), 2010.

From a statistical point of view   137

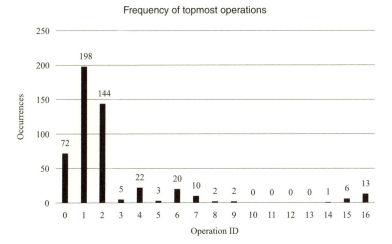

Figure 5.2: Repartition of the topmost decomposition operations for the first Chinese characters taught at TUAT's international center.

required topmost decomposition operations for each of the 45 steps of the learning process. Here, each step corresponds to one lesson, with lessons being successively conducted in step order. The topmost decomposition operation repartition is given in Figure 5.2.

Note that the listed 500 characters actually include five duplicates (話, 電, 早, 遅, 顔), thus totaling 495 distinct characters. The character 々 is the sole one not included in the 2,136 regular-use Chinese characters in Japanese.

Table 5.3: The first Chinese characters taught to foreign students at the Tokyo University of Agriculture and Technology and their topmost decomposition operations – Part I.

Step	Characters															Operation IDs
1	日	月	木	山	田	人	口	車	門							0
2	火	水	金	土	子	女	学	生	先	私						0, 1, 2
3	一	二	三	四	五	六	七	八	九	十	百	千	万	円	年	0, 2, 3, 7, 15, 16
4	上	下	中	大	小	本	半	分	力	何						0, 1, 2, 16
5	明	休	体	好	男	林	森	間	畑	岩	糸					1, 2, 7
6	目	耳	手	足	雨	竹	米	貝	石	糸						0, 1
7	花	茶	肉	文	字	物	牛	馬	鳥	魚						0, 1, 2
8	新	古	長	短	高	安	低	暗	多	少						0, 1, 2
9	行	来	帰	食	飲	見	聞	読	書	話	買	教				0, 1, 2, 7, 15
10	朝	昼	夜	晩	夕	方	午	前	後	毎	週	曜				0, 1, 2, 4
11	作	泳	油	海	酒	待	校	時	言	計	語	飯				0, 1
12	宅	客	室	家	英	薬	会	今	雪	雲	電	売				2
13	広	店	度	病	疲	痛	屋	国	回	因	開	閉				3, 6, 7
14	近	遠	早	遅	道	青	晴	静	寺	持	荷	歌				0, 1, 2, 4
15	友	父	母	兄	弟	姉	妹	夫	婦	彼	若	主	奥	忙		0, 1, 2, 6, 16
16	元	気	有	名	親	切	渡	通	利	不	若	早	忙			1, 2, 5, 6
17	出	入	乗	降	着	渡	通	内	走	歩	止	動	働			0, 1, 2, 4, 6, 9
18	右	左	東	西	南	北	外	住	所	駅	話	社	院			0, 1, 2, 6, 7, 15
19	地	鉄	工	場	公	都	府	県	島	京	電	番	号			0, 1, 2, 3
20	市	町	村	区	都	府	県	島	京	様	答	宿				1, 2, 4, 5, 6, 8
21	練	習	勉	強	研	究	留	質	問	題	科	数	医			1, 2, 4, 7
22	政	治	経	済	歴	史	育	化	理	科	数	医				1, 2, 6, 8
23	映	画	写	真	音	楽	料	組	思	色	白	赤	黒			0, 1, 2, 9

Table 5.4: The first Chinese characters taught to foreign students at the Tokyo University of Agriculture and Technology and their topmost decomposition operations – Part II.

Step	Characters	Operation IDs
24	起 寝 遊 立 座 使 始 終 貸 借 返 送	0, 1, 2, 4, 6
25	結 婚 離 席 欠 予 定 洋 式 和 活 涼	0, 1, 2, 5, 6
26	春 夏 秋 冬 暑 熱 寒 冷 暖 温 涼　　天	1, 2
27	仕 事 者 運 転 選 記 議 員 商 業　　農	1, 2, 4, 16
28	良 悪 点 正 違 同 適 当 難 受 落 残 味 念	1, 2, 4, 7
29	試 験 面 接 説 果 合 洗 流 消 決 念	0, 1, 2
30	指 折 払 投 打 深 相 談 連 絡 決	1
31	旅 約 案 準 備 機 関 局 由 取 求 願 路 泊 特 急	1, 2, 4
32	線 発 到 交 営 自 由 服 相 談 連 信 路 故 注 意	1, 2, 6, 7
33	押 引 割 具 器 個 自 用 服 産 紙 取 辞 求 報 知 誌	0, 1, 2, 16
34	台 窓 具 用 価 産 服 紙 期 辞 集 忘 告 驚	0, 1, 2, 15
35	銀 資 品 個 価 産 笑 顔 別 眠 苦 並 考	1, 2, 6
36	心 感 情 悲 泣 曲 笑 脱 別 集 並 喜	0, 1, 2
37	伝 代 呼 重 燃 軽 狭 弱 眠 苦 並 単 放 喜 驚	1, 2, 16
38	細 太 重 軽 狭 弱 眠 苦 成 簡 単 放	1, 2
39	空 港 飛 階 建 向 設 完 成 野 風 放 橋	0, 1, 2, 4
40	位 置 横 向 原 平 野 風 訪 顔 両 橋 歯	0, 1, 2, 6, 7, 15
41	老 族 配 術 調 必 要 民 類 得 進 顔 歯	0, 1, 2, 4, 14
42	卒 論 実 変 要 続 過 得 以 失 現 礼	1, 2, 16
43	増 加 減 対 賛 共 直 表 制 美 初	1, 2, 4
44	比 較 最 反 対 非 的 性 法 制 課	0, 1, 2, 6, 15
45	全 最 無 非 第 的 性 法 制 課	0, 1, 2

140   *Character Algebra: Going Beyond Relations*

One can thus see, from the data presented in Tables 5.3 and 5.4, that the first characters taught in this case to the foreign students of TUAT are covered by a subset of the operations defined in Section 5.2 and that, moreover, they reflect the repartition obtained from the analysis of the topmost decomposition operations of all the 2,136 regular-use Chinese characters in Japanese, as given in Figure 5.1. One significant difference though is the higher proportion of ϕ_0 operations. This can be easily explained by the fact that the characters included in the radical set $\hat{\mathbb{J}}$, in other words, the characters of the set $\mathbb{J} \cap \hat{\mathbb{J}}$, are among the first characters to be taught, due to their relative simplicity or common usage, and possibly as part of other more complex characters. The fact that the characters of $\hat{\mathbb{J}}$ are by definition all prime completes the explanation of the higher proportion of ϕ_0 operations in this particular scenario.

Bibliographical notes

1. Early character decomposition work was conducted by Osamu Fujimura and Ryohei Kagaya in the article "Structural patterns of Chinese characters" published in the proceedings of the Conference on Computational Linguistics, pages 1–17, Sånga-Säby, Sweden, September 1–4, 1969.

2. Several theoretical aspects of character decompositions

Bibliographical notes   141

have been discussed by Richard Sproat in his book "A computational theory of writing systems" (Cambridge, England: Cambridge University Press, 2000).

3. One can find interesting character sequences exposing character relations and their possible decompositions in the book "Creating a dictionary" (字書を作る, in Japanese) by Shizuka Shirakawa (Tokyo, Japan: Heibonsha (平凡社), 2002). For the algebra proposed in this chapter, we have also relied on the book "Regular-use characters discussion" (常用字解, in Japanese) by the same author for character analysis (Tokyo, Japan: Heibonsha (平凡社), 2003).

4. John DeFrancis also gives insightful information on Chinese characters, their derivatives, and character composition in his book "Visible speech: the diverse oneness of writing systems" (Honolulu, HI, USA: University of Hawaii Press, 1989).

5. The character memorization issue has been extensively discussed in the literature. Contributions include Stephen Richmond's "A re-evaluation of kanji textbooks for learners of Japanese as a second language" (Journal of the Faculty of Economics, Kanto Gakuin University, 15:43–71, 2005), Oreste Vaccari and Enko Elisa Vaccari's "Pictorial Chinese-Japanese characters: a new and fascinat-

ing method to learn ideographs" (Tokyo, Japan: Charles E. Tuttle Company, 1958), Kenneth G. Henshall's "A guide to remembering Japanese characters" (Tokyo, Japan: Charles E. Tuttle Company, 1988), and Yoshiko Mori, Kumi Sato, and Hideko Shimizu's "Japanese language students' perception on kanji learning and their relationship to novel kanji word learning ability" (Language Learning, 57(1):57–85, 2007). The original work "Remembering the kanji, volume 1: a complete course on how not to forget the meaning and writing of Japanese characters" (Honolulu, HI, USA: University of Hawaii Press, 2010) by James W. Heisig based on "imaginative memory" and short stories for Japanese is also a noticeable reference. Similar works by the same author can also be found for simplified Chinese ("Remembering simplified hanzi, volume 1: how not to forget the meaning & writing of Chinese characters," Honolulu, HI, USA: University of Hawaii Press, 2012) and traditional Chinese ("Remembering traditional hanzi, volume 1: how not to forget the meaning & writing of Chinese characters," Honolulu, HI, USA: University of Hawaii Press, 2012) characters. Moreover, Anne Castelain notably proposed another, innovative classification attempt in her book "Direct access instant kanji dictionary" (Tokyo, Japan: Nichigai Associates (日外アソシエーツ), 1998).

Bibliographical notes 143

Finally, the author of this book has also conducted his own research on this subject. Examples include the two articles "Japanese characters cartography for efficient memorization" (International Journal of Computers and their Applications, 21(3):170–177, 2014) and "An implementation of Japanese characters cartography as a learning tool" (Information Engineering Express, 1(1):10–19, 2015). Furthermore, premises regarding character algebra can be found in the article by the same author "Premises of an algebra of Japanese characters," published in the proceedings of the International C* Conference on Computer Science & Software Engineering, pages 79–87, Yokohama, Kanagawa, Japan, July 13–15, 2015.

6. The relationship between character decomposition and Chinese character teaching has been discussed by Shoichi Yokoyama in "Recognition units of characters" (文字の認知単位, in Japanese) published in the proceedings of the National Institute for Japanese Language and Linguistics (NINJAL) Forum, pages 22–26, Tokyo, Japan, September 11, 2011.

7. Linking schema theory to education in the particular case of Chinese characters has been discussed by Richard C. Anderson et al. in "Use of partial information in learning

144   *Character Algebra: Going Beyond Relations*

to read Chinese characters" (Journal of Educational Psychology, 95(1):52–57, 2003) and "Development of morphological awareness in Chinese and English" (Reading and Writing, 16(5):399–422, 2003).

8. Addressing Chinese characters for children's education, Ovid J. L. Tzeng et al. extended the discussion on character structure to psycholinguistics as presented in "Language processing in Chinese" (Amsterdam, Netherlands: North-Holland, 1992) and "The handbook of east Asian psycholinguistics: Volume 1, Chinese" (Cambridge, England: Cambridge University Press, 2012).

9. The Wada fonts illustrating the usage of prime characters and automatic processing are described in the work of Tetsurou Tanaka, Yuichiro Ishii, Mikio Takeuchi, and Eiiti Wada, entitled "Sharing skeleton data by multiple kanji fonts through programmable rendering" (in Japanese) and published in the transactions of the Information Processing Society of Japan, 36(1):177–186, 1995.

CHAPTER 6

Ontological Discussion

It is important to recognize that this whole book is actually an extensive ontological discussion regarding Chinese characters. The objective of this chapter is to formalize the ontological discussion conducted in this book, and more generally as well, regarding these characters. The first section is dedicated to the presentation of a formal information model for Chinese characters. This model will be concretely illustrated in the second section, with various object instance examples.

6.1 Information model

"system"

The discussion of this section relies on the Unified Modeling Language (UML) and, more precisely, the class diagram it defines, so as to describe the information model proposed for Chinese characters. Stated simply, a class describes the properties of an object that instantiates the class, and class associations describe the relations between class instances (i.e., objects). The class diagram given in Figure 6.1 is that of a Chinese character and, importantly, from an international point of view. A class is represented by a box, and class relations are denoted by lines and arrows, depending on the relation type. The diagram is justified below, and concrete examples are given in the next section.

First and foremost, the diagram is centered around the Character class, which is linked to multiple other classes. As such, it is important to note that the properties of a Chinese character are described by the whole diagram and not only the Character class. Next, the various classes defined are discussed together with the various relations (class associations) they induce. An arrow denotes a one-way association, a black lozenge denotes a composition association (used to indicate that the included class cannot exist without the including one), and a white one denotes an aggregation association (used to indicate that, this time, the included class can exist without the including class, that is, can

Information model 147

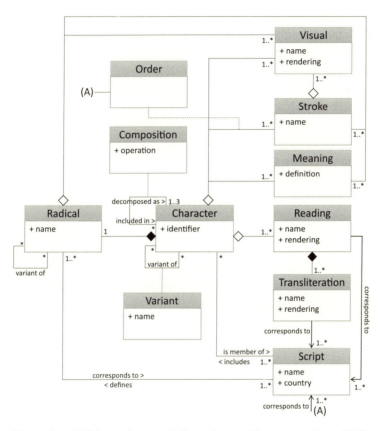

Figure 6.1: A Chinese character information model represented as a UML class diagram.

148   *Ontological Discussion*

be included by other classes). A simple line denotes a two-way association, including labels for each direction when needed.

The Character class includes an identifier field, which is typically used by computer systems to easily identify and distinguish characters. This is the character encoding issue. There exist several different encodings: JIS, Unicode, Big5, EUC, etc. Character encoding is also discussed in Chapter 7. This class has two self-associations. First, there is the Composition association. As seen previously, a character may be the combination of several other characters. Decomposition operations have up to three operands, and, because of the identity decomposition operation, a character can be decomposed as itself, hence inducing the 1..3 arity of the Composition self-association. The Composition class itself has one algebraic operation (see Chapter 5). Next, there is the Variant self-association. As detailed in Section 4.3, a character may have various forms, with each variant thus having a name (e.g., "ancient form," "orthodox form"). While some characters have none, others have multiple forms.

Next, the other associations of the Character class are discussed. First, a character has one unique radical, inducing the association between the Character and the Radical classes. A radical has a name, and the same radical can be obviously used for several characters. As the Character class, the Radical class has a self-association, labeled "variant of." Just as a character, a radical may have variants (refer, for example, to Table 3.6). A radical corresponds to a particular script, has at least one visual

Information model   149

rendering, meaning, and stroke. A script defines its own set of radicals.

A character is made of at least one stroke, has at least one meaning, one visual rendering, and one reading. It is a member of at least one script, and a script includes an undefined number of characters. Regarding visual renderings, each has a name (e.g., "seal"). As for readings, each has a name, which depends on the considered script (e.g., "kun," "on" for Japanese). A reading has at least one transliteration, which has its own name as well and which corresponds to at least one script (e.g., "pinyin" for Chinese). A script has a name and a country. A stroke has at least one visual rendering. Finally, it is interesting to note that one character can have several meanings. Effectively, even though a character may have originally had a unique meaning, the usage of the same character in different dialects, countries, and eras has often contributed to the appearance for that character of new meanings, which may be completely unrelated as seen in Section 2.4.

The Character–Reading association is an aggregation, since the same reading can be used for several, distinct characters. The Character–Visual, Character–Stroke, and Character–Meaning associations are also aggregations, since visuals, strokes, and meanings can exist on their own without the corresponding character instance. The Character–Stroke association is specified by the Order class, which determines the stroke order (i.e., writing order) of the character. It is recalled that the

150 *Ontological Discussion*

writing order depends on the script considered. The Reading–Transliteration association is a composition since a transliteration corresponds to one unique reading. The Stroke–Visual association is an aggregation since it might be possible that the same visual is used for another purpose, like for a character (and not for a stroke). For instance, the visual for the horizontal stroke *héng* can also be used as a visual for the character 一 "one." The same holds for the Radical–Visual association. For instance, the visual for the radical 馬 "horse" can also be used as a visual for the character 馬 (which is indeed at the same time a radical and a character, e.g., 馬 ∈ ℐ ∩ ℐ̂).

6.2 Object instance examples

"precedent,"
"example"

Several concrete examples of object instances with respect to the character information model presented in the previous section are given hereinafter. These examples are presented with a conventional object-oriented programming style of writing (a.k.a. the dotted notation), as used in Java and C++, concretely relying on the dot "." to access the various properties of an object. In addition, it is assumed that all class members are implicitly instantiated. By convention, the member instance name is the member name written in lower case. For example, a Character object has an

Object instance examples   151

instance of the Radical class that is named `radical`. When there is a case of several instances of the same member, they are simply denoted with a number suffix, such as `meaning1`, `meaning2` for the Meaning class.

First, a basic instantiation of the Character class is illustrated. The radical name in this example is derived from Japanese.

```
Character c
c.meaning.definition = {belief, trust}
c.radical.name = ninben
c.visual.rendering = 信
```

Next, the focus shifts to the Reading and Transliteration classes. The character is identified by its Unicode number. This example also serves as illustration for the Script class.

```
Character c
c.identifier = 4FE1 // Unicode for 信
c.reading.name = on
c.reading.rendering = ♪4FE1.wav // reading sound data
c.reading.script.name = Japanese
c.reading.transliteration.name = Hepburn_romanization
c.reading.transliteration.rendering = shin
c.reading.transliteration.script.name = Japanese
```

Hepburn romanization is one common transliteration method of Japanese into the Latin alphabet. It was introduced at the end of

152　*Ontological Discussion*

the 19th century by James C. Hepburn as part of his Japanese-English dictionary.[1]

The Composition association is illustrated below. Note here simplified Character instantiation. The `operation` member is relevant only with respect to the `decomposedAs` member. The declaration order (i.e., for which character the Composition association is declared) is important.

```
Character c1(相)
Character c2(木), c3(目), c4(湘)

Composition comp(c1) // composition declared for c1
comp.operation = "+" // applies only to decomposedAs
comp.decomposedAs = {c2, c3} // ordered
comp.includedIn = {c4}
```

Next, usage of the Variant association is detailed. Once again, attention should be paid to the declaration order.

```
Character c1(学), c2(學)

Variant v(c2) // variant declared for c2
v.variantOf = c1
v.name = orthodox_form
```

---

[1] "A Japanese-English and English-Japanese dictionary" (和英英和語林集成), third edition, Tokyo, Japan: Z. P. Maruya, 1886.

Object instance examples   153

An example for characters of different scripts is given next. Note that character variants and graphical representations (visuals) should not be confused. These are illustrated later.

```
Character c1(业), c2(業)
c1.script.name = simplified_Chinese
c1.script.country = {China, Singapore}
c2.script1.name = Japanese
c2.script1.country = Japan
c2.script2.name = traditional_Chinese
c2.script2.country = {Taiwan, Hong-Kong, Macao}

Variant v(c1)
v.variantOf = c2 // c1 is a simplified variant of c2
v.name = simplified_form
```

The next example illustrates non-trivial instances of the Radical class, including radical variants. A copy constructor is conveniently used to instantiate two variant radicals (obviously also applicable to the Character class). Again, radical names are derived from Japanese.

```
Radical r1(水)
r1.name = mizu
r1.meaning.definition = water
Radical r2 = r1 // copy constructor
r2.name = sanzui // change radical name
```

154　*Ontological Discussion*

```
RadicalVariant rv(r2) // radical variant declared for r2
rv.variantOf = r1

Character c(清)
c.radical = r1 // r2 could indifferently be used thanks to rv
```

Finally, several instances of the Visual class are given below for the character 馬 "horse."

```
Character c(馬)
c.meaning.definition = horse

c.visual1.rendering = 𩧋
c.visual1.name = oracle_bone

c.visual2.rendering = 𤛮
c.visual2.name = big_seal

c.visual3.rendering = 馬
c.visual3.name = regular
```

Bibliographical notes

1. An extended abstract for the proposal of an information model for Chinese characters can be found in the article "A scientific approach to Chinese characters: rationale, ontology and application" by A. Bossard and K. Kaneko,

Bibliographical notes 155

published in the proceedings of the International Conference on Computer Applications in Industry and Engineering, pages 111–116, Denver, CO, USA, September 26–28, 2016, and in the article "Chinese characters ontology and induced distance metrics" by the same authors, published in the International Journal of Computers and Their Applications, 23(4):223–231, 2016.

2. Although written in a largely self-explanatory way, understanding this chapter may be facilitated by acquiring basic knowledge of object-oriented programming. A large part of the theory is covered by the Unified Modeling Language (UML, the specification of the UML 2.5 version being accessible on the Object Management Group official website) and usual notations with concrete language examples are given, for instance, in the case of C++ by Bjarne Stroustrup in "The C++ programming language" (first edition, Boston, MA, USA: Addison-Wesley, 1985).

156 *Ontological Discussion*

CHAPTER 7

Applications

We present in this chapter several applications of the scientific approach to Chinese characters as presented in the previous chapters.

7.1 Universal character encoding

As mentioned at the beginning of Chapter 5, the character coding issue is critical. It is currently a research in progress sponsored by the Chinese government. Concretely, this problem is

158   *Applications*

about assigning a unique identifier (e.g., number) to each Chinese character. The critical issue concerns handling of the characters that are not already covered by, say, the Unicode standard.

"whole,"
"total"

Relying on the character algebra presented in Chapter 5, we are able to propose here a simple approach to uniquely identify characters with a number by defining an injective function from a real character set R (see Section 5.1) to $\mathbb{N}$.

First, each of the $\rho = 17$ operations ϕ_i ($0 \leq i < \rho$) defined in Section 5.2 is naturally assigned to the integer i. Second, to each element of the set $\bar{R}$ (i.e., the set of the prime characters for the real set R, or, in other words, the union of the radical set $\hat{R}$ and the support set $\tilde{R}$) is assigned a distinct natural number j with $\rho \leq j < |\bar{R}| + \rho$. This is possible since by Lemma 3, the set $\bar{R}$ is finite.

We assume without loss of generality that k bits are sufficient to represent the previously assigned numbers. For example, define $k = \lceil \log_2(|\bar{R}| + \rho) \rceil$. Hence, we assemble the character code by concatenating binary blocks of k bits. We use the prefix notation for simple and unambiguous character expression and coding. Effectively, the arity of the defined operations ϕ_i ($0 \leq i < \rho$) is fixed, and thus, no parenthesizing is needed.

Formally, a character expression e is defined by recurrence with the prefix notation as follows (using here a BNF writing

Universal character encoding   159

style, the symbol "|" thus denoting an alternative):

$$e = \phi_i \, e_1 \, e_2 \ldots e_n \; | \; e \in \bar{R}$$

with $e_1, e_2, \ldots, e_n$ again character expressions. In other words, a character expression is either the combination of several character expressions according to one decomposition operation of Section 5.2, or one element of the set $\bar{R}$.

Hence, we can define the character coding function h as follows:

$$h(e) = \begin{cases} \#_k(e) & \text{if } e \in \bar{R} \\ \#_k(\phi_i) \, h(e_1) \, h(e_2) \ldots h(e_n) & \text{otherwise*} \end{cases}$$

* Assume wlog. that e of the form $\phi_i \, e_1 \, e_2 \ldots e_n$.

where $\#_k(x)$ denotes the k-bit number assigned to x, with either $x = \phi_i$ for some i ($0 \le i < \rho$), or $x \in \bar{R}$.

E.g. The character 湘 in 𝕁 is expressed in prefix notation as ϕ_1 氵 ϕ_1 木 目. Assume without loss of generality that 氵, 木, and 目 are all assigned to their radical number (starting from 1, then adding ρ), respectively 85, 75, and 109. Assume further that blocks of $k = 8$ bits are used. As a result, the character 湘 is encoded to the binary number

$\underbrace{0000\,0001}_{\text{8-bit block}}$ 0101\,0101 0000\,0001 0100\,1011 0110\,1101

160   *Applications*

Algorithm 3: ENCODING(e, R)

Input: A character expression $e = e_0 e_1 \ldots e_n$ in the prefix notation
    (with possibly $n = 0$) and a real set R.
Result: A binary sequence corresponding to the character
    expression e.

Array $A = \bar{R}$;   // set $\bar{R}$ copied into array
$A = \text{concatenate}([\phi_0, \phi_1, \ldots, \phi_{\rho-1}], A)$;   // array concatenation
Define $A(u)$ the index of the element u in A;

$k = \lceil \log_2(|\bar{R}| + \rho) \rceil$;
$r = 0$;   // binary sequence, initialized with zeros

for $i = 0$ **to** n **do**
$\quad$ $r = r \ll k$;   // bitwise logical left shift by k bits
$\quad$ $r = r \mid A(e_i)$;   // bitwise logical inclusive OR
end

return r

Consequently, a character code can be decoded by pushing onto a stack each k-bit block starting from the right (i.e., considering the character code in postfix notation). An operation can be distinguished from a character in the stack simply by checking if its value is smaller than or equal to ρ. Two algorithms that implement the character encoding and decoding processes described previously are proposed in Algorithms 3 and 4. Note that for the sake of clarity, the mapping between an element and its index as done in Algorithm 3 is implicit in Algorithm

Universal character encoding   161

4. These two algorithms support operations of any arities (e.g., unary, binary, ternary decomposition operations).

Algorithm 4: DECODING(b, n, k)

Input: A binary sequence b consisting of n blocks of k bits each.
Result: The character corresponding to the binary sequence b.

Stack s;
$mask = 2^k - 1$;

for $i = 1$ **to** n **do**
    $e = b$ & $mask$;   // bitwise logical AND
    if $e < \rho$ **then** // e is an operation
        x = arity of e;   // $x \in \{1, 2, 3\}$ as e either unary, binary, or ternary
        for $j = 1$ **to** x **do**
            $e_j = \text{pop}(s)$;
        end
        c = assemble $e_1, e_2, \ldots, e_x$ according to the operation e;
        $\text{push}(c, s)$;
    else // $e \in \bar{R}$
        $\text{push}(e, s)$;
    end
    $b = b \gg k$;   // bitwise logical right shift by k bits
end

return $\text{pop}(s)$

---

162 *Applications*

7.2 Character distance

"distance,"
"interval"

Building on the previously introduced character information model, several metrics that quantitatively establish the distance separating any two Chinese characters are described in this section. Such a character distance metric enables the automatic generation of character chains, which are ordered sequences of characters with pedagogic applications, as presented in the next section. In practice, the distances calculated are real numbers.

The first metrics presented are morpho-semantic distances. They rely on both the morphological and semantic information provided by characters. Morphological information refers, for example, to character decomposition operations, while semantic information refers, for example, to radical and variant information. The last metric is defined differently, relying solely on character decomposition information.

7.2.1 Morpho-semantic distance

Informally, the more significant the relation between the two characters, the lower the morpho-semantic distance value calculated. Conversely, the distance value is high when the two characters share few attributes.

Character distance 163

7.2.1.1 The δ metric

In this section, given any two Chinese characters a and b, the distance metric $\delta(a,b)$ is first described. Concretely, the distance value $\delta(a,b)$ is a positive real number. To state the formal definition, it is necessary to first consider several character properties. There is some flexibility here, as any character property can be used and the number of such properties can vary freely. To give the definition of the δ metric as concretely and simply as possible, without loss of generality the following two character properties are considered:

- the *variant* property, that is satisfied if and only if the two characters are variants of each other (i.e., a is a variant of b, and vice versa);

- the *radical* property, that is satisfied if and only if the two characters have the same radical.

Let p be the number of properties satisfied between the two characters a and b. Since, in this example, the two character properties *variant* and *radical* have been considered, the inequality $0 \le p \le 2$ holds. Next, character decomposition operations, as introduced in Chapter 5, are used in the distance definition as follows. Let $o_{a,b}$ (resp. $o_{b,a}$) be the minimum number of decomposition operations applied to a (resp. b) until a common element (i.e., a sub-character) is obtained for a and b.

164   *Applications*

It should be noted that the value of $o_{a,b}$ (resp. $o_{b,a}$) is minimal at any time. In the case where the characters a and b have no element in common, we define $o_{a,b} + o_{b,a} = \Omega$, with $\Omega \in \mathbb{R}$ being a large positive constant.

Before going further with the definition of the δ distance metric, an example is given with respect to the $o_{a,b}$ notation. Consider the two characters $a = $ 峠 and $b = $ 雫; the two decompositions $a = $ 山 $+ ($上 $\times$ 下$)$ and $b = $ 雨 $\times$ 下 are induced. Hence, it takes two decomposition operations for a, and one single decomposition operation for b before finding the first common element, here concretely 下. Therefore, the two equalities $o_{a,b} = 2$ and $o_{b,a} = 1$ are obtained.

Next, this number of decomposition operations is further refined to exclude the radicals as follows. Consider that the two characters a and b have radicals r_a and r_b, respectively. In the case where the relations $r_a = r_b$, $a \neq b$, $a \neq r_a$, and $b \neq r_b$ are all satisfied, let $\tilde{o}_{a,b}$ (resp. $\tilde{o}_{b,a}$) be the minimum number of decomposition operations applied to a (resp. b) until finding a common element for a and b other than the radical r_a $(= r_b)$. And, if the characters a and b have no element in common except their radical, similarly define $\tilde{o}_{a,b} + \tilde{o}_{b,a} = \Omega$. Otherwise, that is one of $r_a \neq r_b$, $a = b$, $a = r_a$, or $b = r_b$ is satisfied, simply define $\tilde{o}_{a,b} = o_{a,b}$ (resp. $\tilde{o}_{b,a} = o_{b,a}$). Finally, for any character a, define $\delta(a,a) = 0$.

Similarly, an example is given with respect to the $\tilde{o}_{a,b}$ notation. Considering the two characters $a = $ 沽 and $b = $ 沼 of same

Character distance   165

radical $r = \grave{\gamma}$, the relation $a = 沽 = r + (十 \times 口)$ holds, which induces $\tilde{o}_{a,b} = 2$, and the relation $b = 沼 = r + (刀 \times 口)$ holds, which induces $\tilde{o}_{b,a} = 2$.

Consequently, the definition of the δ metric can be stated as follows.

Definition 33. *For any two characters a and b, their distance $\delta(a,b) \in \mathbb{R}$ is defined as*

$$\delta(a,b) = \frac{\tilde{o}_{a,b} + \tilde{o}_{b,a}}{p+1}$$

It should be noted that if the distance $\delta(a,b)$ depends on Ω, it is inevitably of the form Ω/n with $n \in \mathbb{N}^*$, thus allowing for a total ordering of distances. Several examples of distance calculation with respect to the δ metric are given in Table 7.1. In this table, the "variant" and "radical" columns are Boolean values of respective meanings "*a* is a variant of *b*" and "*a* and *b* have the same radical" if the corresponding value is set to "yes," and the respective opposite meanings if set to "no."

7.2.1.2   Property independence and the δ', δ'' metrics

In its definition, the δ metric described previously includes $p + 1$ as denominator to take into account the properties that are shared between the two characters. This denominator may rightfully be deemed unnatural. To address this issue, two new

166   *Applications*

Table 7.1: Illustrating character distance calculation with the δ metric.

a	b	variant	radical	p	$\tilde{o}_{a,b}$	$\tilde{o}_{a,b}$	$\delta(a,b)$
洪	浜	no	yes	1	2	2	2
榎	夏	no	no	0	1	0	1
桜	櫻	yes	yes	2	2	2	4/3
湘	眼	no	no	0	2	1	3
峠	雫	no	no	0	2	1	3
木	林	no	yes	1	0	1	1/2
木	水	no	no	0	Ω		Ω
沐	浴	no	yes	1	Ω		$\Omega/2$

metrics, δ' and δ'', are introduced in this section. These refine the original δ metric by handling shared properties differently.

For the sake of simplicity but without loss of generality, as with the δ metric, the two character properties *radical* and *variant* are considered. Obviously, more properties would be handled similarly. Define ε $(0 < \varepsilon < 1)$ as the symbolic constant associated with the *radical* property. Similarly, define φ $(0 < \varphi < 1)$ as the symbolic constant associated with the *variant* property. In practice, these constants will be subtracted from the calculated distance in the event the corresponding property is satisfied. Thus, a shared property induces a shorter distance, which is the intended behavior.

Character distance   167

In addition, it is important to note that the considered properties may not always be independent. Hence, given two character properties p and q of respective symbolic constants c_p and c_q, if $p \Rightarrow q$ holds, then 1) $c_p > c_q$ is induced, and 2) only c_p is subtracted (i.e., not subtracting both c_p and c_q). For example, given two constants ε and φ that, respectively, correspond to the *radical* and *variant* properties, when satisfied the *variant* property induces the *radical* property (indeed, for this discussion we can reasonably assume that a character variant only deals with character shape changes, without consequence on the character radical). Therefore, the relation $0 < \varepsilon < \varphi < 1$ holds. Hence, when calculating the distance between two characters that are variants of each other, only the φ constant is subtracted.

As a result, in Definition 34 below, it can be assumed without loss of generality that the shared properties $p_1, p_2, \ldots, p_k$ of any two characters are independent. The definition of the two distance metrics δ' and δ'' is stated below.

Definition 34. *For any two characters a and b sharing the independent properties $p_1, p_2, \ldots, p_k$, their distance $\delta'(a,b) \in \mathbb{R}$ is defined as*

$$\delta'(a,b) = \tilde{o}_{a,b} + \tilde{o}_{b,a} - \sum_{i=1}^{k} c_i$$

168   *Applications*

and their distance $\delta''(a,b) \in \mathbb{R}$ as

$$\delta''(a,b) = o_{a,b} + o_{b,a} - \sum_{i=1}^{k} c_i$$

with c_i the symbolic constant corresponding to p_i.

Distance calculation examples illustrating property independence and the two newly-defined metrics δ' and δ'' are given in Table 7.2. In this table, the distances previously calculated in Table 7.1 are this time expressed with the δ' and δ'' metrics. The two dependent properties p_1, p_2 corresponding to the *variant* and *radical* properties, respectively, and of symbolic constants $c_1 = \varphi$, $c_2 = \varepsilon$, respectively, are considered. Hence, it is again assumed that the relation $p_1 \Rightarrow p_2$ holds.

7.2.1.3   Discussing the δ, δ', and δ'' metrics

Trade-offs seem inevitable for a morpho-semantic character distance metric. Hence, the pros and cons of the three proposed Chinese character distance metrics δ, δ', and δ'' are now reviewed. First, the original δ metric relies on the $p + 1$ denominator, which may seem unnatural, thus triggering the introduction of the two refined metrics δ' and δ''. Second, regarding the δ'' metric and as shown in Table 7.2, the relation $\delta''(洪,浜) = \delta''(沐,浴)$ holds, which induces some incoherence given that the two sub-characters 共,兵 are closer (i.e.,

Character distance   169

Table 7.2: Examples of character distance calculation with the δ' and δ'' metrics.

a	b	p_1	p_2	$\tilde{o}_{a,b}$	$\tilde{o}_{a,b}$	$\delta'(a,b)$	$o_{a,b}$	$o_{a,b}$	$\delta''(a,b)$
洪	浜	no	yes	2	2	$4-\varepsilon$	1	1	$2-\varepsilon$
榎	夏	no	no	1	0	1	1	0	1
桜	櫻	yes	yes	2	2	$4-\varphi$	1	1	$2-\varphi$
湘	眼	no	no	2	1	3	2	1	3
峠	雫	no	no	2	1	3	2	1	3
木	林	no	yes	0	1	$1-\varepsilon$	0	1	$1-\varepsilon$
木	水	no	no	Ω		Ω	Ω		Ω
沐	浴	no	yes	Ω		$\Omega-\varepsilon$	1	1	$2-\varepsilon$

more related) than the two sub-characters 木,谷. Third, regarding the δ' metric and as shown in Table 7.2, the relation $\delta'(沐,浴) = \Omega - \varepsilon$ holds. In other words, even though the two characters 沐, 浴 have the same radical (氵), their distance involves the Ω constant and is subsequently large. While this may seem disturbing at first glance, coherence is actually retained. Yet, one challenging aspect of δ' is that this metric may not treat character variants fairly enough, that is, not reducing the distance value sufficiently when the two characters are variants of each other. For example, the distance $\delta'(桜,櫻) = 4 - \varphi$ is obtained for the two variant characters 桜 and 櫻, while, for

170   *Applications*

example, the distance $\delta'(峠,雫) = 3$ is obtained for the two, not variants, characters 峠 and 雫, with $\delta'(桜,櫻) > \delta'(峠,雫)$ thus holding. Again, even though this may seem disturbing at first glance given that 桜, 櫻 are variants while 峠, 雫 are not, a certain degree of coherence is retained. For comparison, the original δ metric induces the distances $\delta(桜,櫻) = 4/3$ and $\delta(峠,雫) = 3$. This issue is nonetheless mitigated with the δ'' metric as $\delta''(桜,櫻) = 2 - \varphi$ and $\delta''(峠,雫) = 3$ are obtained.

To summarize this discussion, each of the three distance metrics δ, δ', and δ'' has its own issues. For δ, the denominator may be deemed unnatural, for δ'' some incoherence is induced as explained, and δ' can give the impression of treating variant characters unfairly.

7.2.2   Mathematical distance

The distance metrics δ, δ', and δ'' that have been defined in the previous section are not distances in the mathematical sense of the word. It is indeed easy to show that these metrics do not satisfy the triangle inequality (i.e., the distance relation $\overline{AC} \le \overline{AB} + \overline{BC}$ for a triangle ABC). A new distance metric d that is this time a mathematical distance is proposed in this section. Thus, unlike the previous distance metrics, the d metric satisfies the symmetry property and the triangle inequality. The d metric is related to the Levenshtein distance (a.k.a. edit distance), which is used, for instance, to quantitatively evaluate

Character distance   171

how related two character strings a, b are. Concretely, this is done by counting the minimum number of character operations – such as deletion and insertion – that are required to transform the string a into the string b (hence the name "edit distance"), or vice versa.

First, it is assumed without loss of generality that each character is either a combination of sub-characters or a canonical character (see Section 5.1). For the sake of clarity, only binary decomposition operations are considered. Yet, a similar discussion could be extended to ternary operations. Furthermore, the $\emptyset$ symbol represents the empty character, which is thus canonical (prime). The definition of the d metric is as follows.

Definition 35. *Given two Chinese characters a and b, their distance $d(a,b) \in \mathbb{R}$ is defined as*

$$0 \qquad \text{when } a, b \text{ canonical}, a = b$$

$$1 \qquad \text{when } a, b \text{ canonical}, a \neq b$$

$$\min\{d(a,b_1) + d(\emptyset,b_2),$$
$$\qquad d(\emptyset,b_1) + d(a,b_2)\} \qquad \text{when } a \text{ canonical}, b \text{ not}$$

$$\min\{d(a_1,\emptyset) + d(a_2,b),$$
$$\qquad d(a_1,b) + d(a_2,\emptyset)\} \qquad \text{when } b \text{ canonical}, a \text{ not}$$

$$\min\{d(a_1,b_1) + d(a_2,b_2),$$
$$\qquad d(a_1,b_2) + d(a_2,b_1),$$

172   *Applications*

$$d(a_1,\emptyset)+d(a_2,b),$$
$$d(a_1,b)+d(a_2,\emptyset),$$
$$d(a,b_1)+d(\emptyset,b_2),$$
$$d(\emptyset,b_1)+d(a,b_2)\}\qquad otherwise$$

where a (resp. b) is either canonical or of the form $a = a_1 \bullet a_2$ (resp. $b = b_1 \bullet b_2$), with $\bullet$ a character decomposition operation (see Section 5.2).

Next, it is shown with the following proposition that the d metric is indeed a mathematical distance.

Proposition 1. *The d metric is a mathematical distance.*

Proof. Consider any two characters a and b. Obviously, $d(a,b) \geq 0$ holds.

First, it is shown by mathematical induction that $d(a,b) = 0 \Leftrightarrow a = b$. This is the induction hypothesis. It is proved that this relation holds in the case both a and b are canonical, which is the base case of the induction. Assume $a = b$. Since a is canonical, $d(a,b) = d(a,a) = 0$ can be directly deduced. Assume $d(a,b) = 0$. Since a,b are canonical, by definition the equality $a = b$ holds.

Next, it is shown in the general case that $d(a',b') = 0 \Leftrightarrow a' = b'$ holds with $a' = a \bullet \tilde{a}$, $b' = b \bullet \tilde{b}$, and $\tilde{a},\tilde{b}$ canonical. The case $a' = \tilde{a} \bullet a$, $b' = \tilde{b} \bullet b$ is shown similarly. By definition, and as per the induction hypothesis, $d(a',b') = d(a,b)+d(\tilde{a},\tilde{b}) = d(\tilde{a},\tilde{b})$

Character distance   173

holds. So clearly, $d(a',b') = 0 \Leftrightarrow d(\tilde{a},\tilde{b}) = 0$ and $d(\tilde{a},\tilde{b}) = 0 \Leftrightarrow \tilde{a} = \tilde{b}$.

Second, $d(a,b) = d(b,a)$ is trivial since all the sub-character pair combinations are systematically exhausted by definition. Therefore, a and b can be swapped freely.

Third, it is shown that the triangle inequality $d(a,c) \leq d(a,b) + d(b,c)$ holds for any characters a,b,c. Again, mathematical induction is used. It is proved that this relation holds in the case that a, b, and c are all canonical, which is the base case of the induction. If $a = b = c$, then $d(a,c) = d(a,b) = d(b,c) = 0$ and the hypothesis $d(a,c) \leq d(a,b) + d(b,c)$ is satisfied. If $a = b$ and $a \neq c$, then $d(a,c) = d(b,c) = 1$ and $d(a,b) = 0$, and the hypothesis holds. If $a = c$ and $a \neq b$, then $d(a,b) = d(b,c) = 1$ and $d(a,c) = 0$, and the hypothesis holds. If $a \neq b \neq c$, then $d(a,c) = d(a,b) = d(b,c) = 1$ and the hypothesis holds.

Next, it is shown in the general case that $d(a',c') \leq d(a',b') + d(b',c')$ holds with $a' = a \bullet \tilde{a}$, $b' = b \bullet \tilde{b}$, $c' = c \bullet \tilde{c}$, and $\tilde{a},\tilde{b},\tilde{c}$ canonical. The case $a' = \tilde{a} \bullet a$, $b' = \tilde{b} \bullet b$, $c' = \tilde{c} \bullet c$ is shown similarly. The relation $0 \leq d(\tilde{a},\tilde{b}) \leq 1$ holds since $\tilde{a},\tilde{b}$ canonical. Thus, $d(a',b') \geq d(a,b) + d(\tilde{a},\tilde{b})$ and $d(a',b') - d(\tilde{a},\tilde{b}) \geq d(a,b)$ for any a,b. Hence, by the induction hypothesis, it can

174   *Applications*

be derived that:

$$d(a',c') - d(\tilde{a},\tilde{c}) \leq d(a,c)$$
$$\leq d(a,b) + d(b,c)$$
$$\leq d(a',b') - d(\tilde{a},\tilde{b}) + d(b',c') - d(\tilde{b},\tilde{c})$$
$$d(a',c') \leq d(a',b') + d(b',c')$$
$$+ d(\tilde{a},\tilde{c}) - d(\tilde{a},\tilde{b}) - d(\tilde{b},\tilde{c})$$

It is recalled that $0 \leq d(\tilde{a},\tilde{c}), d(\tilde{a},\tilde{b}), d(\tilde{b},\tilde{c}) \leq 1$ since $\tilde{a},\tilde{b},\tilde{c}$ canonical. Hence, $d(\tilde{a},\tilde{b}) = d(\tilde{b},\tilde{c}) = 0$ holds if and only if $\tilde{a} = \tilde{b} = \tilde{c}$, and thus $d(\tilde{a},\tilde{b}) = d(\tilde{b},\tilde{c}) = 0 \Rightarrow d(\tilde{a},\tilde{c}) = 0$. Therefore, $d(\tilde{a},\tilde{c}) - d(\tilde{a},\tilde{b}) - d(\tilde{b},\tilde{c}) \leq 0$ holds, and

$$d(a',c') \leq d(a',b') + d(b',c')$$

is satisfied.   □

It should be noted that, unlike the previous metrics, the metric d does not rely on character properties, thus encoding less information than δ, δ', and δ''. This is a trade-off required in order to satisfy the triangle inequality. Examples of distance calculation with respect to the d metric are given in Table 7.3. For facilitated comparison, these examples are the same as those of Table 7.1.

The d metric is discussed next. First, the meaning of this distance metric differs from those of the δ, δ', and δ'' metrics.

Character distance 175

Table 7.3: Illustrating character distance calculation with the *d* metric.

a	*b*	$d(a,b)$
洪	浜	$d(氵,氵)+d(共,兵)=d(卅,丘)+d(八,八)=1$
榎	夏	$d(木,\emptyset)+d(夏,夏)=1$
桜	櫻	$d(木,木)+d(妛,嬰)=d(⺍,賏)+d(女,女)=$ $d(⺍,貝)+d(\emptyset,貝)=d(⺍,目)+d(\emptyset,八)+$ $d(\emptyset,目)+d(\emptyset,八)=4$
湘	眼	$d(氵,艮)+d(相,目)=1+d(木,\emptyset)+$ $d(目,目)=2$
峠	雫	$d(山,雨)+d(卡,下)=1+d(上,\emptyset)+$ $d(下,下)=2$
木	林	$d(木,木)+d(\emptyset,木)=1$
木	水	1
沐	浴	$d(氵,氵)+d(木,谷)=1$

Effectively, while retaining character distance coherence, the distance value induced by the *d* metric is completely different. The main reason for this is that the total number of decomposition operations being always counted, two unrelated canonical characters are at distance 1, whereas they are at distance Ω with the previous metrics. The standpoint is simply different: with the *d* metric, the less the number of decomposition operations, the shorter the distance.

176　　*Applications*

Second, regarding the "sharpness" of the d metric, one should note that the d metric is less sharp than the others. In comparison with the δ, δ', and δ'' metrics, multiple pairs of different characters will induce the same distance value with the d metric, while they would have not with the previous metrics. This behavior is symptomatic of the lack of acknowledgment of character properties such as the *radical* and *variant* properties when calculating distance values with the d metric. As an example, consider the equality $d(洪,浜) = d(氵,氵) + d(共,兵) = d(共,兵)$. Instead of counting the first horizontal combination operation and then subtracting a constant induced by the *radical* property (since the two characters 洪, 浜 both have 氵 as radical), the first decomposition operation clearly impacts not the final distance value as it involves the same character. Precisely, the term $d(氵,氵)$ results in 0 as per the definition of the d metric.

7.3　Character chains

In this section, we present a pedagogical application to the character distance metrics previously described: character chains. Concretely, character chains are sequences of Chinese characters that are ordered in such a way that the number of changes between two consecutive characters is minimum. The sequence 单 → 單 → 戰 → 蝉 → 虫 → 蟲 is an informal example of such a character chain: these six characters are ordered such that the memorization effort between any two consecutive characters is minimized. The previously presented character distance metrics enable the formal definition and automatic generation of character chains.

"procession,"
"companion"

Character chain creation is now precisely explained by relying on a concrete example, with a formal character chain generation algorithm eventually being given. The generation of a character chain starts from a finite set of Chinese characters. From a pedagogical point of view, such a set may represent the characters to be learned by students for a certain period of time. Here, we consider the character set $E = \{单, 單, 戦, 蝉, 虫, 蟲\}$, which corresponds to the character chain given earlier as an informal example. In addition to a character set, a starting character $c \in E$ needs to be given as input to initiate the generation of the character chain. The selection of the starting character depends on the application, but is typically a character of rather simple shape, possibly canonical or prime. Here, let c be 单, so as to match the previous character chain example.

The main idea is to recursively iterate the characters of the set E in order to identify the character of $E \setminus F$ that is closest to the current character, where $F \subseteq E$ is the set of the already processed characters (i.e., the characters that are already included in the character chain being generated). The current character is

178   *Applications*

initialized to the starting character c. For the set E and the initial character c previously given, the steps listed below are induced when relying on the δ distance metric. Any distance metric would obviously do, yet the resulting character chain may differ. Each step is given in the form `<step number>`. `<current character>` : `<set of character distances>`, with each element of the set of character distances being a pair $(e \in E, \gamma \in \mathbb{R})$ where the character e is at distance $\delta(c,e) = \gamma$ of the current character c.

1. 单 : $\{(蟲,\Omega),(戰,1),(蟬,1),(虫,\Omega),(單,2/3)\}$

2. 單 : $\{(蟲,\Omega),(戰,3),(蟬,3),(虫,\Omega)\}$

3. 戰 : $\{(蟲,\Omega),(蟬,2),(虫,\Omega)\}$

4. 蟬 : $\{(蟲,1),(虫,1/2)\}$

5. 虫 : $\{(蟲,1/3)\}$

Hence, the character chain 单 $\rightarrow$ 單 $\rightarrow$ 戰 $\rightarrow$ 蟬 $\rightarrow$ 虫 $\rightarrow$ 蟲 is obtained, matching the character chain that was used as an introductory example.

Finally, as a summary, the pseudo-code of a simple recursive algorithm generating such a character chain is given in Algorithm 5.

Algorithm 5: CHAINING(E, c)

Input: An unordered set of characters E and a starting character $c \in E$.

Result: A character chain starting from c and corresponding to the set E.

if $|E| = 1$ **then**
   | **return** c // indeed, $E = \{c\}$
else
   | $E' = E \setminus \{c\}$;
   | $N = \arg\min_{e \in E'} \delta(c, e)$;
   | $\{n_1, n_2, \ldots, n_{|N|}\} = N$;   // c equidistant to n_i ($1 \leq i \leq |N|$)
   | **return** $c \to$ CHAINING(E', n_1)
end

Bibliographical notes

1. Our initial discussion regarding character distance metrics and character chains can be found in the previously-cited articles "A scientific approach to Chinese characters: rationale, ontology and application" (Proceedings of the International Conference on Computer Applications in Industry and Engineering, pages 111–116, Denver, CO, USA, September 26–28, 2016) and "Chinese characters ontology and induced distance metrics" (International Journal of Computers and Their Applications,

180   *Applications*

23(4):223–231, 2016).

2. Character encoding in general is the objective of the Unicode Consortium, which has published several versions of the Unicode standard. The Unicode standard aims at covering the majority of the writing systems known to humanity and is therefore a huge task and specification. The Basic Multilingual Plane (BMP) covers the most frequent Chinese characters used in various languages such as Japanese and Chinese, while a few more infrequent Chinese characters are included in the Supplementary Ideographic Plane (SIP). While earlier versions of the Unicode standard were available in printed form (see for instance "The Unicode 5.0 standard" (fifth edition, Boston, MA, USA: Addison-Wesley, 2007)), recent iterations of the standard are available online on the Unicode Consortium official website.

CHAPTER 8

A Step Further

In this chapter, more advanced discussions regarding Chinese characters are conducted. More advanced also means that these discussions are possibly more subjective and thus liable to debate. However, while the following sections reflect the views of the author, they are supported by numerous arguments and examples in an attempt to demonstrate their soundness.

182   *A Step Further*

8.1   Hinting at the semantics of the 亻 + operation

亻

the *ninben*
radical

In this section, several tracks are explored that hint at the peculiar semantics of the combination operation 亻 + in Japanese, that is, the horizontal combination of the *ninben* element 亻 with another character, in this order. One should note that this is not a linguistic analysis *per se* as it does not include discussion of synchrony and diachrony, or extensive corpus analysis. Yet, the exposed properties of this combination operation are striking enough for the findings to be included in this book.

In Japanese, linguistic modality is conventionally expressed by compounds (verbal or not) such as *ga hitsuyō* to express necessity and *ga dekiru* to express possibility. Here, relying on various analyses and numerous examples, we investigate and exhibit the existence of another, completely different form of modality expression in Japanese. Precisely, we show that such modality emerges from the usage of the *ninben* radical when applied to several Chinese characters used in Japanese with the combination operation 亻 +.

In this study, we will focus on the Chinese characters of radical *ninben* as used in Japanese. This radical has for meaning "man, human," and its main graphical rendering 人 is, notably,

Hinting at the semantics of the イ + operation   183

a pictogram (form of the marching man, the biped). The *ninben* radical can also be found with the renderings イ and 𠆢, with the イ variant being the most common by far and the one relevant for our discussion here. Our objective is to first demonstrate the existence of a modal aspect induced by this *ninben* radical for certain characters (of *ninben* radical). This modal aspect is characterized by the modification of the meaning of the character. Next, we will investigate the meaning of this modality, in other words, the extent to which the meanings of the impacted characters are modified.

In comparison, the Japanese tongue relies on several modal constructions that we call "conventional" to avoid any confusion. From a syntactical point of view, these modalities are expressed either by the usage of a syntagm (often prepositional, sometimes verbal), or by a verbal suffix. We give below several non-exhaustive examples of the expression of modality. First, the alethic modality: possibility is commonly expressed thanks to the syntagm *ga dekiru*, among other available grammatical constructs such as *ga kanō*. For the expression of necessity, the syntagm *ga hitsuyō* is frequently used. These modal constructs are hardly distinguished from conventional prepositional (or verbal) syntagms. Nonetheless, possibility can also be expressed with the verbal suffix *-eru*. For the deontic modality, obligation is expressed mainly with the verbal suffix *-naito ikenai* (and its variants), and the verbal suffix *-beki* for moral duty. Regarding the epistemic modality, the expression of certitude

184   *A Step Further*

is obtained by usage of the syntagm *no hazu*, and that of uncertainty by usage of the suffix (not necessarily verbal) *-sō*. Finally, for the subjective modality, the expression of will is realized either with the verbal suffix *-[i]tai*, or with the syntagms *ga hoshii* and *ga iru*.

It should be recalled that any study with respect to Chinese characters and their meanings can hardly be dogmatic given the complexity, history, and evolution ("syntactic" (morphological) and semantic) of these characters. For this reason, we will always try to support our propositions and affirmations with concrete and sufficiently documented examples.

This section is organized as follows. The proposition of modality induced by the *ninben* radical as analyzed in this study is presented in Section 8.1.1. Then, Section 8.1.2.1 is dedicated to the study of multiple concrete character cases that illustrate the proposal from diverse angles. In Section 8.1.2.2, we will present the semantics of this modality as extracted from the obtained results. A tentative counting of the characters of *ninben* radical that are concerned by our proposition will be undertaken in Section 8.1.2.3. We will show in Section 8.1.3 that this modal aspect of the *ninben* radical is indeed specific to this radical. The Section 8.1.4 is dedicated to the refutation of various hypothesizes with respect to the role of the *ninben* radical in the considered examples. Precisely, the simplification hypothesis and the pronunciation hypothesis will be successively discussed. Finally, a short conclusion to this study will be given in Section

Hinting at the semantics of the イ + operation   185

8.1.5.

8.1.1   Analytic approach

In this section, we present our proposition and analytic approach regarding the modal aspect induced by the *ninben* radical for certain characters.

As previously explained, we will focus on the characters of *ninben* radical and, more precisely, on those horizontally combining *ninben* + rest. For the sake of clarity, let us denote by $A = N + c$ these characters, where the constant N simply designates イ (*ninben*), and c the variable part on the right of *ninben* when considering the original character A. These notations are in accordance with those of Section 5.

These characters of the form $N + c$ make up the vast majority for the *ninben* radical. Indeed, they approximatively account for 243 out of a total of 258 characters of *ninben* radical (statistics based on the *Kadokawa shinjigen* dictionary[1]), character variants excluded (note that this difficult topic of character counting is treated in more detail in the next section), that is more than 94%. The characters 仏, 儚, and 働 are some examples of these characters of the form $N + c$. We thus have, for $A = 働$, the equality relation $c = 動$.

We state our proposition as follows: it appears that some of

---

[1] 角川 新字源, revised edition, Tokyo, Japan: Kadokawa (角川), 1994.

186　*A Step Further*

the characters of the form $A = N + c$ retain the meaning "without *ninben*," in other words, the meaning of c, meaning which is however modulated, even though slightly, when using in a word (i.e., a group of Chinese characters whose combination induces a particular meaning) the character in its version "with *ninben*" (i.e., the usage of A as is).

Let us be more precise. If we consider the initial meaning of the character A (i.e., the meaning of the character A on its own and not that of A when used in a word), we rediscover in one way or another, having possibly to go back to a lost or infrequently used original meaning, a relation with the meaning of the *ninben* radical: "man, human." But when reusing this character A inside a word, such a relation to the human is lost, and only the meaning of the character c, that is "without *ninben*," is retained.

This proposition is illustrated with the following two examples.

Example 1
The word 仲町 "town of the middle." The character $A =$ 仲, with thus $c =$ 中, here has the meaning of "middle, central," which is also the meaning of the character 中, and therefore that of c. The *ninben* radical is present in A, but at first glance without being necessary.

Example 2

Hinting at the semantics of the 亻 + operation   187

The word 仔犬 "puppy (baby dog)." The character $A = $ 仔, with thus $c = $ 子, here has the meaning of "child" (literally, 仔犬 has for meaning "child of dog"), which is also the meaning of the character 子, and therefore that of c. Once again, the *ninben* radical is present in A, but at first glance appears to be unnecessary.

In the next section, we will conduct a detailed analysis to document this proposition, involving various examples of characters of *ninben* radical.

8.1.2 Census, analysis, and semantics

8.1.2.1 Case study: representative characters

In this section, several characters of *ninben* radical that are representative of this study are collected and analyzed, in other words, characters of the form $A = N + c$, with N the 亻 (*ninben*) constant, whose meanings when used inside a word are those of c.

The character 仲 is one of the most representative characters in this study. It has already been presented as an illustration of our proposition in the previous section. Its main meaning includes the sense of cadet, precisely the child who is between the eldest and the youngest. We rediscover here the literal meaning of the character: "the one of the middle." In this case, we thus have $c = $ 中 "middle." The words containing this character that

188   *A Step Further*

validate our proposition include 仲町 for "town of the middle," which is a popular town (district) name, and 仲見世 for "[the district of] stalls of the middle" (this word is an obsolete synonym of 商店街 "merchant district," but is still found in several Japanese cities, such as Kawasaki and Tokyo's Asakusa). The translation of this second example, 仲見世 *nakamise*, is nontrivial and may thus be subject to discussion. The more ancient appellation of the Asakusa Nakamise district,[2] 平店 *hiramise*, might give a hint since holding a clear meaning of positioning (平 "surface, flat"). Let us give two last examples for this character: 仲通り for "main avenue" (literally "avenue of the middle"), and 仲村 for "village of the middle," the latter example being used as a family name, long ago designating the location of the house inside the hamlet. Once again, these words are examples of the usage of a character A of meaning c.

The character 仔 is also an example representative of our study and has been used to illustrate our proposition previously. Its usual meaning includes the sense of "young, childish." With this character, we thus have $c = $ 子 "child." Words including this character that validate our proposition include 仔犬 "puppy (baby dog)" and 仔猫 "kitten (baby cat)" (and also 仔牛, 仔馬 for "veal" and "foal," respectively). Another clue with this character is its pronunciation within these words, in *ko* instead of the

---

[2]Asakusa Nakamise Promoting Union, 2008. Refer to http://www.asakusa-nakamise.jp.

Hinting at the semantics of the 亻 + operation 189

usual pronunciation in *shi* or *sai*, which reinforces the assimilation of 仔 in 子 given that the character 子 is also, and mainly, read *ko*.

The character 价 has the meaning of "kindness." It has for particularity that the character $c = $ 介, one meaning of which being "independent, alone" (when dealing with a person), is also of *ninben* radical (yet not of the form $N + c$). Our proposition is applied to this character for instance with the word 貴价 "a man of high [social] rank" inside which one can identify the meaning of the character 价 as "a lone [man]," that is the meaning of 介, the character 貴 meaning "high [social] rank." Effectively, the two words 貴价 and 貴介 are given as synonyms ("synonym" here and after standing for similar meaning, not exactly identical), which corroborates our proposition.

Next, let us look into certain characters of *ninben* radical that feature, in addition to their usual utilization, a very particular usage: quantifiers. These characters include, for example, 伍, 什, 佰, and 仟, which initially designate the chief of a five, ten, hundred, and thousand men troop, respectively, with the military being the main domain of application. Effectively, we have 五 "five," 十 "ten," 百 "hundred," and 千 "thousand."

These quantifiers are actually highly interesting for our study. For example, let us cite the *Daijirin* dictionary[3] at the 大字 *daiji* entry: "「一・二・三」などの代わりに用いる

---

[3] 大辞林, third edition, Tokyo, Japan: Sanseido (三省堂), 2006.

190   *A Step Further*

「壱・弐・参・肆・伍・陸・漆・捌・玖・拾・佰・阡」 などの字。金銭証書などに用いる。" This definition teaches us that the character 伍 has, among others, indeed the meaning of five as is, without any relation to man. This definition also allows us to make the same remark for the character 佰 and hundred. Furthermore, one should note that this definition is that of the word 大字, literally "big [important] character." Thus, this way of counting with these particular characters (壱, 弐, 参, 肆, 伍 for one, two, three, four, five, respectively, instead of the conventional 一, 二, 三, 四, 五) grants additional importance to the numbers. This is why, as mentioned in the second part of the dictionary definition, these particular characters are used, for example, for the numbers on bank notes. This information is very valuable as it will help us to identify and specify the modal sense of *ninben* in the rest of this chapter (Section 8.1.2.2). Besides, for the sake of precision, one should note that the special quantifiers (i.e., non-conventional) for ten and thousand are 拾 and 阡, respectively, and not 什 and 仟 as it could have been assumed. This does not, at any rate, invalidate our discussion.

Finally, to conclude this topic on quantifiers, it is also interesting to note that in the case of the character 什 and its usage inside the word 什器 "furniture," this sense of multiplicity is retained ($c = 十$ "ten"), but, and thus validating our proposition, without any relation to man (i.e., *ninben*).

This case study is wrapped up by giving the following examples which also illustrate our proposition.

Hinting at the semantics of the 亻+ operation   191

First, let us cite the character 俚 "common people," and its usage in the word 俚婦 "rural woman." Besides, we have $c =$ 里, "country (rural area), village," and 婦 "woman," hence once again exhibiting this modality induced by the *ninben* radical. Effectively, the two words 俚婦 and 里婦 are given as synonyms. This analysis of the character 俚 is supported by a second example perhaps even more clearly. This second example concerns the word 俚閭 "the gate of the village." One can see directly with this word that the meaning of the character 俚 is that of the character 里: "village."

One of the meanings of the character 供 is "preparation," meaning which is also found with the character $c =$ 共. The character 供 inside the word 供具 (a utensil for Buddhist religious rituals) has thus the same meaning as 共, "preparation," which once again shows a certain modality. Effectively, the two words 供具 and 共具 are given as synonyms.

As another example, the character 侈 "luxury" is found inside the word 華侈 "luxurious." We have $c =$ 多 "multitude," which indeed reflects the literal meaning of 華侈: "multitude of splendors."

The character 係 "[the person, or being] in charge" is found in the word 係数 "coefficient" (mathematics). We have here $c =$ 系 "who/which puts into relation," clearly showing the literal meaning for coefficient: "number which puts into relation." The meaning of the character 係 in the word 係数 is thus indeed that of c.

192   *A Step Further*

The character 傀 "big," but also "strange," is included in the word 傀儡 "marionette." Besides, we have the character 儡 for "fallen [in disgrace], come down to." We have here $c = $ 鬼 "imp, creature." From these two meanings for the characters 儡 and 鬼, one can easily deduce the literal meaning of this word: "fallen [to the state of marionette] imps," and conclude reasonably that the meaning of the character 傀 inside the word 傀儡 is indeed that of c.

The character 伸 "lengthen, stretch" is found inside the word 追伸 "*post scriptum*." Besides, we have the character $c = $ 申 "comment, announce," clearly illustrating in the word 追伸 the usage of the character $A = $ 伸 with the meaning of c.

The character 仁 "wisdom" is used inside the Buddhist word 仁王, which designates the two guardians – literally "kings," usually translated as "guardian gods" – in the form of statues (仁王像) who guard at the gate of the temple (split on the left and right sides of the gate). An illustration is given in Figure 8.1. We find again the meaning of $c = $ 二 "two," and thus the character $A = $ 仁 used with the meaning of c.

We give three last examples that give a different point of view in comparison with the previously mentioned characters and which are based on the same idea. The character 乍 is the original form of the character 作 "create, make" (Shirakawa, 字統, p. 357) and was thus used in various words and expressions such as 寝を乍る "to make for oneself a place to sleep" with the meaning of the actual character 作, in other words,

Hinting at the semantics of the イ + operation   193

Figure 8.1: The two imposing guardian gods (仁王 statues) who stand at the gate of the Tenrinji Buddhist temple in Hamamatsu (天林寺, Hamamatsu, Shizuoka, Japan).

where modern Japanese would use 作. This example showing the semantic evolution <c toward A> (from a semantic viewpoint, one could then very well use c as is without combining it to *ninben*), this character is thus actually another representative of our study: A used with the meaning (here original) of c, *ninben* being in this case an addition of modern Japanese. Similarly, the character 賞 "reward" is the original form of the char-

194   *A Step Further*

acter 償 "compensation" (Shirakawa, 字統, p. 469), and was thus used in this way, that is, with the current meaning of the character 償. Finally, the character 立 "standing" is the original form of the character 位 "position" (Shirakawa, 字統, p. 15), and was thus used for example in the expression 立に即く "fixedly positioned" with the current meaning of the character 立. One can find again, perhaps fortunately, traces of this ancient synonymy in the mathematical syntagm "neutral element," which can be translated in Japanese with the two words 単位元 and 中立元. Notice here the conjugated usage of the characters 立 and 位.

Multiple other characters are subject to becoming suitable examples. Yet, it is sometimes difficult to detect such occurrences because of the very close, possibly identical, meanings of *A* and *c* (or at least the residual meaning that made it to us), as for instance with the characters 偵 and 貞.

8.1.2.2 Semantics

Our proposition having been supported by several and diverse examples (see Section 8.1.2.1), it is now time to think about how to characterize this modality induced by the *ninben* radical for multiple characters inside numerous words, in other words, which meaning to confer on it. Again, this is a difficult task, and as such, the rest of Section 8.1.2.2 should be regarded as a hypothesis (mostly consisting of two propositions), tentatively

Hinting at the semantics of the 亻 + operation   195

supported by several examples.

A first hint, and probably the most robust, to address this modality semantics issue was spotted in the previous section when analyzing several special quantifiers. This is our first proposition: the fact of using inside a word the character A (i.e., "with *ninben*"), whereas just using the character c (i.e., "without *ninben*") would do (the meaning is the same), adds more weight (importance) to the word thus constituted. This proposition has been clearly illustrated by the special quantifiers (大字) such as 伍 "five" and 佰 "hundred." As another example, the district name 中町 is relatively hollow, meaning "the town of the middle," but in a rather tasteless way. On the contrary, the district name 仲町 shows more weight and even more depth. This first interpretation is arguably applicable to all the characters that validate our original proposition (see Section 8.1.1), such as the characters 仔, 价, and 供.

Next, let us refine this interpretation. This is our second proposition: despite the risk of losing generality (this second interpretation will not be necessarily applicable to all the characters that validate our original proposition, even though applicable to the majority of the previously reviewed characters), it appears that combining *ninben* with a character confers on this character not only more importance, but also a social dimension. This is not really surprising as the *ninben* radical has indeed the meaning "man." Nonetheless, this does not invalidate the fact that the character retains its meaning "without *ninben*." For ex-

196   *A Step Further*

ample, where the word 中町 conveys the idea of position of the town (in the middle), using instead the word 仲町 adds this social aspect while retaining the simple meaning of "town of the middle." It is important to note that we do not get back to the original meaning of the character 仲, which would invalidate the pertinence and interest of our study. In the case of a simple addition of the radical meaning to the rest of the character, we would get back directly to the definition of the compound ideograph character class (see Section 3.2). For example, with the word 仔犬 "puppy (baby dog)," the "living" aspect of the puppy is emphasized more than the parent–child relation induced by the writing 子犬 of this same word "puppy." Similarly, regarding the character 价 and as explained previously, the character 介 is of radical *ninben*, and thus the idea of "man" is already present in *c*. By further combining it with *ninben*, the social dimension of the resulting character 价 is augmented.

Finally, it should be noticed that the examples of words using this modality of characters of *ninben* radical are found in dictionaries rather parsimoniously. Effectively, using or even playing with this modal aspect, such words are common for proper nouns (places, persons). Note here that the proper nouns in Japanese have clearly established meanings, unlike for instance in French (at least modern), and that it is at times difficult to distinguish between proper and common nouns.

Hinting at the semantics of the 亻 + operation   197

8.1.2.3   Counting

In this section, our objective is to quantitatively evaluate the frequency of this modal aspect when considering as exhaustively as possible the set of characters of *ninben* radical. Toward this aim, it is first necessary to count the number of characters of *ninben* radical, which is far from trivial for the same reason that the number of existing Chinese characters remains unknown, and also because of a lack of dogmatism regarding character classification. In fact, for some characters, it is still unclear what their radicals are, and such characters can thus be classified differently from one reference to another, as shown previously in Section 3.3. Next, we tentatively propose an estimation of the number of characters of *ninben* radical that reflect the discussed modal aspect. Once again, this is not an easy task since it is difficult to analyze all the possible candidates given their large number. Finally, it is necessary to exclude particular characters of *ninben* radical since being not of the form $A = N + c$, that is, whose morphologies differ from "*ninben* on the left, the rest on the right," the character 今 being an example of such character to be excluded.

We have reviewed the totality of the 258 characters of *ninben* radical (as per the *Kadokawa shinjigen* dictionary) and have assigned to them a type in the form of an integer in the range from 0 to 3 as follows:

Type 0   character of *ninben* radical that does not hold the con-

198 *A Step Further*

sidered modal aspect;

Type 1 character of *ninben* radical that validates our proposition;

Type 2 character of *ninben* radical with the meaning of *A* and that of *c* being very close, or even identical, and the character *A* thus possibly validating our proposition;

Type 3 character of *ninben* radical but not of the form $N + c$.

The details of this analysis are given in Table 8.1. Columns are labeled "C" for character and "T" for type.

The data in Table 8.1 are summarized in Figure 8.2. One can see that in total, more than 29% of the characters of *ninben* radical are likely to reflect the discussed modal aspect, and with 20% of those having their modal aspect shown in this analysis. These results are indeed significant.

8.1.3   A specificity of the *ninben* radical

The aim of this section is to show that the modal aspect exposed in this study is specific to the *ninben* radical. First, it is important to note that even if some characters such as 沖 "open sea" and 鰯 "sardine" combine the meanings of their radicals (here, respectively, 氵 "water" and 魚 "fish") and those of the remaining character parts – such a character is thus of the compound ideograph class (see Section 3.2) – here, respectively, 中 "middle"

Hinting at the semantics of the イ + operation 199

Table 8.1: Classification of the characters of *ninben* radical.

C	T	C	T	C	T	C	T	C	T	C	T	C	T	C	T	C	T	C	T	C	T	C	T
人	3	化	0	介	3	仇	0	今	3	什	1	仍	2	仁	1	仄	3	仆	0	仏	0	仂	2
以	3	仡	0	仕	2	仔	1	囚	3	仗	0	刧	2	仙	0	仟	0	他	0	代	0	付	0
令	3	伊	0	仮	0	会	3	价	1	企	3	伎	2	休	0	伋	0	仰	0	件	0	伍	1
伉	2	伈	0	仲	1	伝	0	任	2	作	1	伺	2	佌	0	伏	0	仿	0	佚	2	何	0
伽	2	佔	0	佝	0	佐	2	佃	2	佔	0	伯	0	佌	0	似	0	住	0	佗	2	但	0
佇	0	体	0	低	0	佾	0	価	0	佳	0	佽	0	伾	0	佖	0	佈	2	伻	0	佑	0
余	3	伶	0	依	0	佟	1	価	0	侍	0	侏	2	佗	0	侂	0	佶	0	供	1	血	0
佼	2	使	1	侈	1	攸	2	佯	1	侏	2	侂	0	侅	0	侚	1	侠	0	佩	0	佪	1
侮	0	併	2	侔	2	侑	0	侁	0	来	3	例	0	俞	3	俄	0	俅	0	俠	0	俚	0
係	2	俔	0	俣	0	侯	0	俟	0	俑	0	俎	3	俏	2	信	0	侵	0	促	0	俗	0
偮	0	俘	0	便	0	俛	0	保	0	俑	0	俚	1	俐	0	侶	0	俤	0	俥	0	候	0
倚	0	倭	0	俺	0	俱	0	俶	0	俱	0	倔	2	倪	2	倹	0	倬	0	個	0	値	2
倖	2	倥	2	倅	2	借	0	俳	0	倡	2	俾	0	倩	0	倩	0	倦	0	倓	0	倮	0
倀	0	偶	0	倒	0	俳	0	偓	0	偶	0	俵	0	府	0	做	0	倅	0	們	0	偈	0
倞	0	倆	2	倫	0	偲	0	偍	0	偶	0	偃	2	偝	0	修	0	偽	0	偶	0	偉	0
健	0	偲	0	偖	0	偲	0	側	0	偸	0	停	2	偵	2	偪	0	偏	0	偭	2	傾	0
傀	1	廉	0	微	0	傞	0	傘	3	傖	0	備	0	傅	2	傍	2	傴	0	僅	0	傾	0
傑	2	傲	0	債	0	催	0	傷	0	僉	3	僦	0	僧	0	僄	0	傭	2	僂	0	働	0
們	0	僖	2	僦	0	僑	2	僥	0	僦	0	僭	0	像	0	僅	2	僕	0	僚	0	億	0
儈	0	儀	2	僵	0	儕	0	儆	0	償	0	儕	0	詹	0	儂	0	儡	0	債	2	僻	2
儗	2	儒	0	盡	0	儕	0	儔	0	儜	0	儐	0	夢	2	償	1	儩	0	優	0	儡	0
儲	0	傯	0	儺	0	儷	0	儼	2	儻	2												

and 弱 "weak," this idea of modality by the radical as revealed in this study for the *ninben* radical is not present. Effectively, the two character examples 沖 and 鰯 are not used inside words with the meaning of *c*, "middle" and "weak," respectively.

200   *A Step Further*

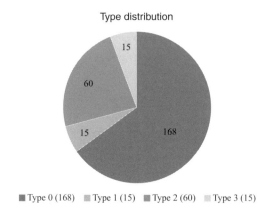

Figure 8.2: Distribution of the types of the characters of *ninben* radical.

Because it would be clearly impractical to analyze all the characters of all the radicals, we will review the characters of *gyōninben* radical. This radical has been selected from the 213 others (i.e., 214 minus *ninben*) as it has significant similarities with the *ninben* radical. Indeed, several characters of *ninben* radical of the form $A = N + c$ have meanings close to those of the corresponding characters $A' = G + c$ with $G = 彳$ (*gyōninben*). For example, the word 俳佪 has the same meaning as the word 徘徊, precisely "wander." Thus, the *gyōninben* radical is a satisfactory representative of the other radicals for a meaningful

Hinting at the semantics of the 彳 + operation   201

comparison with the *ninben* radical, the modal aspect discussed being more likely, at least as likely, to appear in the case of the *gyōninben* radical than with other radicals.

Just as we did with the study of the *ninben* radical, we will consider only the main form of the characters of *gyōninben* radical, their variants (if any) not being considered in this analysis. In total, 33 characters of *gyōninben* radical have been accounted for (once again as per the *Kadokawa shinjigen* dictionary). Several types for the characters of *gyōninben* radical are similarly distinguished:

Type 0 character of *gyōninben* radical that does not hold a modal aspect similar to that identified for the *ninben* radical;

Type 1 character of *gyōninben* radical that holds a modal aspect similar to that identified for the *ninben* radical;

Type 2 character of *gyōninben* radical with the meaning of A' and that of c being very close, or even identical;

Type 3 character of *gyōninben* radical but not of the form $G + c$ (c not empty).

The details of this analysis are given in Table 8.2. Columns are labeled "C" for character and "T" for type. For the sake of clarity, the data in Table 8.2 are summarized in the diagram of Figure 8.3.

202   *A Step Further*

Table 8.2: Classification of the characters of *gyōninben* radical.

C	T	C	T	C	T	C	T	C	T	C	T	C	T	C	T	C	T	C	T	C	T
彳	3	彴	0	役	0	彷	2	往	0	徑	0	征	0	徂	0	低	0	彼	0	後	0
很	0	徇	2	待	0	律	0	從	0	徐	0	徒	0	徙	0	徜	2	得	0	徘	0
御	0	徨	0	循	0	復	0	徯	0	微	0	徭	0	徵	0	德	0	徹	0	徽	0

First, one will notice a clear difference between the repartition of the types of the characters of *ninben* radical and those of *gyōninben* radical. Where the modal aspect revealed in this study is found in multiple characters of *ninben* radical (Type 1), it is totally absent in the case of the *gyōninben* radical. Furthermore, as discussed next, it can also be affirmed that Type 2 is negligible, not to say absent (see details below), in the case of the *gyōninben* radical.

Effectively, regarding Type 2, it is interesting and important to note that in all the cases where a character of *gyōninben* radical, say $A' = G + c$, is of Type 2, it appears that actually this character A' is at least assimilable to (e.g., 彷), even in some cases directly a variant of (e.g., 徇), the character $A = N + c$. For example, the character of *gyōninben* radical 彷 is of Type 2. This character is often assimilable to the character of *ninben* radical 仿. It can thus be reasonably suggested that such a character of *gyōninben* radical (A') is of Type 2 because of its assimilation to the corresponding character of *ninben* radical (A), and therefore that no character of *gyōninben* radical is really of

Hinting at the semantics of the 亻 + operation 203

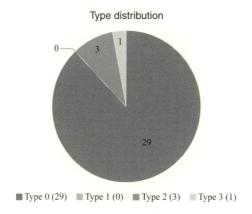

Figure 8.3: Distribution of the types of the characters of *gyōninben* radical.

Type 2.

8.1.4 Other (refuted) hypotheses

8.1.4.1 A simplification of characters?

History, and in particular 20th century history, has witnessed in several countries governmental reforms aiming at simplifying the usage of Chinese characters, Japan (1949, refer to the table of the regular-use *kanji* characters (当用漢字表) by the Japanese Ministry of Education, The Agency for Cultural Affairs

204   *A Step Further*

(1946)) and China (1956) in the first place, with notably for objective to lower the illiteracy rate, which was particularly high in China then (for instance, in comparison with that of Europe at the time). Concretely, the simplification of characters induced the usage of a lesser number of strokes for particular characters. Hence, numerous characters exist in (at least) two variants: the traditional form and the modern form, for instance 學 and 学 for "study, learning."

Such a process of simplification, thus regarding the morphology of a character, cannot pretend to explain the usage of *ninben* when it is not directly necessary as described previously. Effectively, the presence of *ninben* is not compatible with character simplification since the character *A* is logically more complex (i.e., includes more strokes) than the character *c*. Note that the reverse situation, that is the semantic evolution <*A* toward *c*> could, however, be subject to discussion, but this is not the point of our study.

8.1.4.2   *Ninben* added for pronunciation?

As explained in Section 3.2, Chinese characters can be classified into six classes depending on their morphologies. The phonosemantic compounds combine two distinct parts: one part induces semantic information (i.e., information about the character meaning), and the other part pronunciation information. For example, the reading of the character 銅 "bronze" is induced

Hinting at the semantics of the 亻 + operation 205

by its right part 同 while semantic information is induced by the left part 金 "metal" (and also "money," by extension). A large majority of Chinese characters are phono-semantic compounds, and inside these, the characters of the form $x + y$ are the most frequent, either x or y possibly being the character radical, depending on the character. Thus, it is easy to see that the characters considered in this study, that is of *ninben* radical and of the form $A = N + c$, are mostly phono-semantic compounds, the *ninben* radical inducing semantic information, and c the right part of the character inducing pronunciation information.

In general, and particularly for the case of phono-semantic compounds, it is extremely rare, if not impossible (we were not able to find a single example, but it is always difficult to be dogmatic when dealing with Chinese characters) for the pronunciation of a character to be induced by its radical (of course, except if the character itself is a radical). In other words, in general, and particularly for the case of phono-semantic compounds, the pronunciation of a character A of radical k is induced by $A \setminus \{k\}$ the part of the character that does not include k. In our case, that is for characters of *ninben* radical, it is easy to see that we are in the general case: the *ninben* radical does not induce character pronunciation information. It is also easy to verify this assertion: we list in Table 8.3 the main readings (*on* and *kun*, the infrequent readings being omitted) of the characters mentioned in this study. One can directly notice that these readings are distinct from those of the *ninben* radical, precisely *nin* / *jin*, in 95%

206   *A Step Further*

Table 8.3: The main pronunciations of the characters given as examples in this study of the modal aspect of the *ninben* radical.

Character	*on* reading	*kun* reading
仲	*chū*	*naka*
仔	*shi, sai*	-
价	*kai*	*yo, yoro*
伍	*go*	-
什	*shū, jū*	-
佰	*haku, byaku*	*osa*
仟	*sen*	*kashira*
俚	*ri*	*iya, hina*
供	*kyō, ku*	*sona, tomo*
侈	*shi, i*	*ogo, ō, hiro*
係	*kei*	*kaka, tsuna*
傀	*kai*	*ō, kugutsu, deku*
伸	*shin*	*no*
仁	*jin, ni, nin*	-
作	*saku, sa*	*tsuku, na*
償	*shō*	*tsuguna*
位	*i*	*kurai*

Hinting at the semantics of the 亻 + operation   207

of the cases, the unique exception being the character 仁. We can thus reasonably conclude that these readings are induced exclusively by c.

8.1.5   To summarize

In Section 8.1, we discussed the *ninben* radical of Chinese characters, a particular case of radical for which we have exposed the modal aspect in Japanese. Through the study of several characters and their usages in Japanese, we were able to specify, even tentatively, the meaning of this modality. Our findings rely on several concrete examples of words (i.e., combinations of characters) that support our proposition. Out of 258 characters of *ninben* radical accounted for (as per the *Kadokawa shinjigen* dictionary), 29% are likely to present the modal aspect discussed in this study, the modal aspect of 20% of these characters having been shown in this analysis. Also, several hypotheses that could have invalidated our proposition – absolutely legitimate hypotheses – have been discussed and consequently refuted. Precisely, it has first been shown that the case of the *ninben* radical is a particular case, the other radicals not holding such a modal aspect. For that, the *gyōninben* radical has been selected, which is a particular radical since it is more strongly linked to *ninben* than other radicals and thus more likely to include the modal aspect presented. The obtained results clearly show that the *gyōninben* radical does not hold this modal aspect. Then, the hypothesis of possible influence from character simplification as witnessed by history several times, in Japan (1949) and China (1956) for example, has been discussed and consequently refuted. Finally, it has been shown that the presence of the *ninben* radical is not related to the pronunciation of the considered characters.

It would be interesting to expand this *ninben* study to Chinese. Since Japanese is originally based on the same characters as those used in Chinese, it would be natural to first investigate whether such a property is also found in Chinese, second to identify the radicals concerned, and third to discuss the differences noticed with respect to this property between the two languages.

8.2 Simplification reforms

"simplicity,"
"oneness"

The character simplification reforms as previously mentioned for Japan and China have induced new character elements (sub-characters) while aiming at simplifying character reading and writing, and that mostly by reducing the number of strokes included in the characters. Hence, from an algebraic point of view (refer to Chapter 5), these reforms often complicate character morphological understanding by introducing new decomposition patterns, precisely new elements

Simplification reforms 209

Table 8.4: Illustrating several new character patterns induced by character simplification reforms.

Orthodox	Simplified	Description
觀	観	One new element (雚) vs. existing ones: 艹, 口, 隹.
險	険	One new element (㑒) vs. existing ones: 一, 口, 人.
畫	画	One new element (甶) vs. existing ones: 聿, 田, 一.
竝	並	One new character (並) vs. an existing one: 立.

in the support set of the considered language, that is, for instance, feeding the set $\tilde{\mathbb{J}}$ in the case of Japanese. Concrete examples of new patterns induced by character simplification are given in Table 8.4. The orthodox and simplified forms of a character are given with an explanation of the newly-induced elements.

The examples of Table 8.4 are selected from Japanese. A similar discussion can be held for the case of Chinese: the simplified character 见 induces a completely new character while the traditional form 見 is the combination of the two existing elements 目 and 儿.

210   *A Step Further*

It is thus often easier to algebraically decompose orthodox forms rather than simplified ones, adding a new element into the support set or a completely new character into the real set inducing a highest penalty. For instance, consider the simple expression 竝 $=$ 立 $+$ 立 $= 2$立 induced by the orthodox form, versus the fact that the simplified form 并 induces a completely new character, which is thus assigned a high penalty since increasing the memorization load on the learner.

In addition, it is important to mention that because of character simplification, the simplicity of character classification according to radicals has been significantly deteriorated. Effectively, after simplification, a character may not exhibit its radical at all. For example, consider the character 竝 (orthodox form). Its radical is 立, and its simplified form is 并. Hence, considering the simplified form, it would definitely be unnatural to state that the character is of radical 立, and the learner would have to exclusively resort to memorization for radical identification, which is obviously impractical and against the radical classification principles. Because of this grotesque situation, the radical of the simplified form 并 has been set to 一. A similar discussion can be made with the character 兩 (orthodox form) of radical 入 and whose simplified form 两 not including 入 as a sub-character any more has seen its radical also changed to 一. Furthermore, the radicals of several simplified characters remain highly debated. Simplification is indeed one reason for the lack of dogmatism regarding character classification based

Simplification reforms   211

on radicals.

Moreover, prohibitively, as illustrated in previous chapters, character simplifications are almost always specific to one language. Hence, by relying on simplified characters, the huge merit of sharing logograms, and thus words that are often cognates, across languages is severely harmed. As a result, it is common that Japanese people are not able to understand Chinese words, let alone characters, because of simplifications. And the opposite can also be verified: Chinese people often experience severe difficulties when trying to understand Japanese words, let alone characters, again because of simplifications local to Japan, or, conversely, simplifications that were made in China and not in Japan. If China and Japan had retained the exclusive usage of orthodox characters, the degree of understandability between the two writing systems would have undoubtedly been significantly increased, and in addition, understandability with Korean would have been partly (i.e., Hangul being in the way) retained as Korea has not introduced simplification reforms, as explained previously.

The character simplification issue has been extensively discussed in the literature, for instance regarding the simplification reform of Japanese, with many authors emphasizing the difficulties introduced by the reform – and thus being highly dubitative of its soundness – thereby corroborating the challenges and issues induced by character simplification as presented earlier in this section with respect to character relations and algebra. For

212   *A Step Further*

example, in the case of Japanese, Itsuhei Aoki in his book "Old *kanji*, old *kana* proficiency"[4] describes how paradoxically confusing and counter-productive simplified characters can be in comparison to their traditional forms. Even though traditional form characters include a higher number of strokes, their readability and memorization is not more difficult, and it can well be the opposite that holds. As recognized by Aoki, one drawback of old forms compared against new forms is that even though the *Kāngxī* dictionary characters were the consensus, old form characters may lack homogeneity, in other words, the multiplicity of possible writings for one same character is cumbersome (e.g., the three variants 叙, 敘, 敍 of the same character as mentioned by Tetsuji Atsuji,[5] the former variant having been retained as the new form).

Finally, it is interesting to note that paradoxically, documents written with orthodox forms instead of simplified ones remain easily readable thanks to contextual information. Numerous examples could be cited, but the modern (post-simplification reform) Japanese book "My Japanese language school" by Tsuneari Fukuda written with orthodox forms is a good example. It can thus be reasonably assumed that simplified forms are not for easier reading but rather for facilitated writing. Thus, one

---

[4]旧字力、旧仮名力 (in Japanese), Tokyo, Japan: NHK Publishing (NHK 出版), 2005.

[5]"*Kanji* history in post-war Japan" (戦後日本漢字史, in Japanese), Tokyo, Japan: Shinchosha (新潮社), 2010.

could wonder why creating new forms (i.e., simplified forms) from scratch (e.g., 並) since there already exist in most cases vulgar forms whose precise purpose is to be used for unofficial, rapid writing. Even if using those for informal writing, official writing would still be done with orthodox forms, which is not problematic since it is not casual writing, and sufficient care and resources can thus be allocated to redaction.

8.3 The case of Chữ nôm

ba, "three" in Chữ nôm

In this section, the main morphological properties of local Chữ nôm characters are reviewed. As mentioned in Section 2.4, most characters that are local to Chữ nôm realize the combination of two existing Chinese characters, resulting in most cases in phono-semantic compounds, and otherwise, rather frequently in semantic compounds. Very rare are the local Chữ nôm characters that consist in modified Chinese characters, such as the local Chữ nôm character 伩 *ấy*, which is derived from the Chinese character 衣. These exceptional local Chữ nôm characters that are modified Chinese characters are not addressed in this section.

The following two morphological properties of local Chữ nôm characters can be noticed.

First, in most cases, if not all, the new characters introduced

214 *A Step Further*

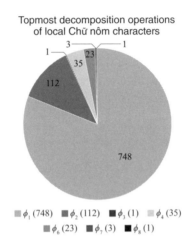

Figure 8.4: Repartition of the topmost decomposition operations of local Chữ nôm characters.

by Chữ nôm have one single additional layer. That is, for instance, the horizontal combination of two existing Chinese characters or their vertical combination.

Second, the repartition of the topmost decomposition operations (refer to Chapter 5) of local Chữ nôm characters is given in Figure 8.4. One should note that this account is based on the Taberd dictionary and that it is sometimes difficult to identify the topmost operation. Hence, these results should be seen as a

Bibliographical notes 215

trend, which is anyway very clear: most local Chữ nôm characters combine existing Chinese characters with the ϕ_1 and ϕ_2 operations, thus reflecting the trend noticed previously for Chinese characters in general.

In addition, one may note that the ϕ_4 operation is the third most-used topmost decomposition operation. In most cases, the ϕ_4 operation can be interchanged with the horizontal combination operation – this interchangeability of the two operations ϕ_4 and ϕ_1 is noticed for Chinese characters in general. For example, the character 㠟 could also be similarly written as 巴＋三 without impacting the readability or correctness of the writing. This second writing for this particular example can be seen, for instance, on the second page of the 1901 Chữ nôm book "*Bảo xích tiện ngâm*" (保赤便吟) within the word 㠟辢 *ba năm* "three years"; see Figure 8.5 (courtesy of the Vietnamese Nôm Preservation Foundation[6]).

Bibliographical notes

1. Character simplification in the case of Japanese is presented in an easy-to-read manner in the book "Introduction to old *kanji* and old *kana*" (旧字旧かな入門, in Japanese) by Mitsuo Fukawa and Kazuo Koike (Tokyo, Japan: Kashiwashobo (柏書房), 2001).

---

[6] Digital library VNPF Id NLVNPF-0521, Origin Id R.1954.

216   *A Step Further*

2. The *ninben* radical study was supported in particular by the dictionary *Jitō* (字統) of Shizuka Shirakawa (Tokyo, Japan: Heibonsha (平凡社), 1984), and by the extensive reference dictionary *Daikanwa jiten* (大漢和辞典) of Tetsuji Morohashi (Tokyo, Japan: Taishukan Publishing (大修館書店), 2000).

3. The soundness of Japanese simplification reforms, including those for the Japanese *kana* script, are passionately discussed and questioned in the book "My Japanese language school" (私の國語教室, in Japanese) by Tsuneari Fukuda (Tokyo, Japan: Shinchosha (新潮社), 1960, Tokyo, Japan: Bungeishunju (文藝春秋), 2002).

Bibliographical notes 217

Copyright Vietnamese Nôm Preservation Foundation

Figure 8.5: Illustrating the $\phi_4 \leftrightarrow \phi_1$ assimilation of local Chữ nôm characters with the character 呰 (occurrence in the center column).

218   *A Step Further*

CHAPTER 9

Toward Practice

Throughout this book, we have presented, reviewed, and analyzed Chinese characters, and that from a global point of view, that is, considering various languages and writing systems. The reader should thus at this point have gained a deep understanding of what Chinese characters are, how they are formed, and how they relate to each other. Hence, the reader has now acquired important knowledge that will support further Chinese character studies, with character memorization being most probably the next task to be faced. This is facilitated now that character classes, morphologies, and relations have been studied.

220   *Toward Practice*

So, as an epilogue for the present work, the author will suggest below with books several paths that would consist in the next steps for the reader wishing to continue exploring the fascinating world of Chinese characters. Some of these books may have already appeared in bibliographical notes from previous chapters. To begin, several references regarding character memorization are given.

Already mentioned in previous bibliographical notes, the three-volume book "Remembering the kanji" by James Heisig[1] is a best-seller. It deals with Chinese characters as used in Japanese. For each character (especially in the first volume), a short, sometimes poetic, story is given, aiming at providing the learner with mnemonic tools for character memorization. The first volume is dedicated to remembering the meaning and writing of characters, the second to character reading with respect to Japanese, and the third to reading and writing characters at an advanced level. Volumes 2 and 3 tend to be character lists though.

For example, Heisig often structures his story for a given character around the several elements (called primitives therein) of the character, relying on the respective meanings of these primitives, possibly assigning to primitives altered meanings for clarity. It should be noted that this approach is only a mnemonic as, in fact, relying for memorization on the seman-

---

[1] Honolulu, HI, USA: University of Hawaii Press, 2010 (latest editions).

Toward Practice 221

tics of each character element separately cannot be applied to phono-semantic compounds, obviously. So, now that the reader has acquired knowledge regarding character relations, it would be interesting to expand the analysis proposed by Heisig by further linking characters together, possibly deriving new stories as mnemonics.

These books by Heisig have been completed by the same author to address simplified Chinese: "Remembering simplified hanzi," and traditional Chinese: "Remembering traditional hanzi," both being in two volumes.[2]

Numerous books aimed at supporting Chinese character memorization could be cited here, but, as mentioned in previous chapters, such books more or less inevitably end up listing characters with meaning, phonetic, and possibly other information, so the previous references of this nature are enough for now. However, because their approach is rather different, let us nonetheless mention that elementary school textbooks as used, for instance, in Japan provide interesting and often well-illustrated ways to learn characters, usually starting with pictograms and associated short explanatory sentences. Obviously, such textbooks are not aimed at the foreign learner, but the reader might find it enjoyable to go through them.

To wrap up the character memorization topic, the author cannot resist citing dictionaries which have been of great help

---

[2]Honolulu, HI, USA: University of Hawaii Press, 2012 (latest editions).

222   *Toward Practice*

for the present work, and the study of Chinese characters in general. Chronologically, the *Shuōwén jiězì* dictionary (説文解字; 2nd century) is, even though not very accessible, interesting for its classification system of 540 radicals as well as for explanations regarding the six writing character classification. Several books provide help for reading the *Shuōwén jiězì* dictionary, for example the "*Shíyòng shuōwén jiězì*" work by Ke He Zang and Ben Cai Liu,[3] which goes through the characters, their writing styles, meanings, and morphologies as used in the original dictionary. The 7th–8th century *Ganlu zishu* (干禄字書) character reference work is surprisingly absorbing, as it gives valuable information on the actual usage of characters in earlier centuries, precisely showing the orthodox form of a character along with several variants and their respective acceptability. The early modern *Kāngxī* dictionary (康熙字典; 18th century) is also very interesting since, featuring the modern 214 radicals, it allows for comparison with the ancient *Shuōwén jiězì* dictionary. These two old dictionaries are still widely accessible with frequent reprints, at least in China.

Modern dictionaries and reference books include the acclaimed and extensive *Daikanwa jiten*[4] in twelve volumes, the

---

[3] 實用説文解字 (in Chinese), Shanghai, China: Shanghai Guji Chubanshe (上海古籍出版社), 2003.

[4] 大漢和辞典, Tokyo, Japan: Taishukan Publishing (大修館書店), 2000.

Toward Practice   223

Daishogen[5] and the *Nihon nanji itaiji daijiten*[6] for comprehensive analysis regarding character variants and styles, and the *Tự điển chữ nôm dẫn giải*[7] which proposes exhaustive work on the Chữ nôm characters. Last but not least, the general audience dictionaries on Chinese characters such as the *Kadokawa shinjigen* dictionary[8] are most probably the books to which the reader will resort most of the time.

Next, leaving the character memorization topic aside, it should be noted that a scientific approach similar to the one proposed in this book could be applied to other writing systems, Tangut being an example. For further information and comparison, various writing systems of humanity, thus including Chinese characters, are reviewed for example by Florian Coulmas in his book "The writing systems of the world,"[9] by John De-Francis in his book "Visible speech,"[10] and by Geoffrey Sampson in his book "Writing systems."[11]

Still regarding the logical approach to writing systems, the book "A computational theory of writing systems" by Richard

---

[5] 大書源, Tokyo, Japan: Nigensha (二玄社), 2007.

[6] 日本難字異体字大字典, Tokyo, Japan: Yushikan (遊子館), 2012.

[7] Saigon, Vietnam: Social Science Publishing House, 2014.

[8] 角川 新字源, revised edition, Tokyo, Japan: Kadokawa (角川), 1994.

[9] Oxford, England: Basil Blackwell, 1989.

[10] Honolulu, HI, USA: University of Hawaii Press, 1989.

[11] Sheffield, England: Equinox Publishing, 1985, second edition in 2015.

224   *Toward Practice*

Sproat[12] gives an insight into computational linguistics, formalizing and analyzing, for instance, phonetic information and orthography of various languages and writing systems, including Chinese characters. Furthermore, to master character morphologies and relations, it would also be very valuable for the learner to practice character algebra, for example in the form of a game by considering equations of Chinese characters. Concretely, as detailed in the article "Extending the algebra on Japanese characters to equations,"[13] the aim is to solve a linear equation. For this, omitting details, inverse operations need to be defined for the decomposition operations of Chapter 5, for instance, say $\overline{+}\cdot$ and $\cdot\overline{+}$ for the left and right inverses of the $+$ operation, respectively, and say $\overline{\times}\cdot$ and $\cdot\overline{\times}$ for the left and right inverses of the $\times$ operation, respectively. Relying on these operations and considering the domain $\mathbb{J} \cup \hat{\mathbb{J}}$, the case of an equation with a single unknown is exemplified below with the character 茄 "aubergine."

---

[12]Cambridge, England: Cambridge University Press, 2000.

[13]Proceedings of the International Conference on Computer Applications in Industry and Engineering, pages 83–88, San Diego, CA, USA, October 12–14, 2015.

$$^{\text{艹}} \times (力 + x) = 茄$$
$$^{\text{艹}}\,\overline{\times}\cdot \left(^{\text{艹}} \times (力 + x)\right) = {^{\text{艹}}}\,\overline{\times}\cdot 茄$$
$$力 + x = {^{\text{艹}}}\,\overline{\times}\cdot \left(^{\text{艹}} \times 加\right)$$
$$力 + x = 加$$
$$力\,\overline{干}\cdot (力 + x) = 力\,\overline{干}\cdot 加$$
$$x = 力\,\overline{干}\cdot (力 + 口)$$
$$x = 口$$

The above equation and its resolution may be rather straight-forward. Yet, beyond the deduction of the value of the unknown *x*, this exercise illustrates well the point that was addressed in this book: the learner should practice Chinese characters to better understand their morphologies. Such practice then becomes a great support when confronting the challenging task of character memorization. Chinese character description and further analysis have been conducted in the previous chapters in order to provide as much information as possible to this end. By relying on such training, learning characters will be an enjoyable activity, which is after all the key to successful studies.

"end"

APPENDIX A

Topmost Decomposition Operations

We give in Tables A.1, A.2, A.3, A.4, and A.5 the topmost decomposition operations, as presented in Section 5.2, for all the 2,136 regular-use Chinese characters (+5 that were later excluded from the official list), as defined in Japanese (常用漢字). The characters are ordered from left to right in accordance with the official regular-use character list, as published by the Japanese Ministry of Education. Columns are labeled "C" for Character and "O" for operation.

Table A.1: The topmost decomposition operations for the regular-use Chinese characters in Japanese – Part I.

C	O	C	O	C	O	C	O	C	O	C	O	C	O	C	O	C	O	C	O	C	O	C	O
亜	15	哀	15	挨	1	愛	15	曖	15	悪	2	握	1	圧	6	扱	2	宛	2	嵐	2	安	2
案	2	暗	1	以	1	衣	0	位	0	囲	3	依	8	彙	1	委	2	威	2	為	2	畏	2
胃	2	尉	1	異	2	移	1	萎	1	偉	2	医	4	茨	2	意	2	違	4	維	3	慰	3
遺	4	緯	1	域	2	育	2	一	2	壱	3	椅	1	隠	2	芋	1	引	6	印	1	因	0
咽	1	姻	1	員	2	院	1	淫	1	陰	1	逸	2	永	1	韻	1	右	2	宇	1	羽	2
雨	0	唄	1	鬱	13	畝	2	浦	1	運	2	飲	6	益	2	泳	2	英	1	映	1	越	2
営	2	詠	1	影	1	鋭	1	衛	2	易	4	雲	2	宴	1	液	2	駅	3	悦	3	完	1
謁	1	閲	7	円	4	延	1	沿	1	疫	1	怨	2	奥	1	媛	1	援	1	園	16	喚	1
猿	1	遠	4	鉛	1	塩	1	演	14	炎	2	艶	2	価	2	王	1	凹	1	央	1	漢	1
往	1	押	1	旺	6	欧	2	殴	1	縁	2	音	1	渦	2	温	2	穏	1	屋	14	観	1
憶	1	臆	1	虞	5	乙	0	俺	1	桜	2	佳	1	牙	1	果	1	河	1	下	1	願	1
火	0	加	1	可	1	仮	1	何	1	卸	1	貨	2	快	1	過	2	我	1	苛	1	亀	1
架	2	夏	2	家	2	荷	1	華	1	花	2	蚊	1	階	2	瓦	1	改	2	暇	2	輝	1
靴	1	寡	1	歌	1	箇	1	稼	1	菓	1	会	1	崖	2	戒	1	楷	1	画	1	犠	2
悔	1	海	1	餓	2	介	1	回	1	課	1	害	1	革	1	塊	1	街	1	怪	1	急	1
壊	2	懐	1	骸	1	皆	1	械	1	灰	2	角	1	甘	2	涯	1	格	1	核	1	居	1
該	1	概	1	較	1	貝	1	外	1	絵	1	喝	1	患	1	獲	2	学	2	岳	2	叫	1
郭	1	覚	1	掛	1	垣	1	柿	2	劾	1	干	1	寛	2	喚	2	葛	1	寒	1	胸	1
額	1	顎	1	株	7	釜	2	閣	1	各	1	乾	1	館	1	頑	1	汗	1	感	1	仰	1
轄	1	且	1	冠	1	棺	1	括	1	確	1	閑	1	眼	1	奇	1	貫	1	祈	1	金	0
肝	1	官	1	敢	1	巻	1	鎌	6	刈	1	憾	1	旗	1	器	1	幹	1	規	1	銀	1
堪	1	換	1	関	1	歓	1	間	1	陥	1	岩	1	逆	1	虐	1	環	5	畿	5		
慣	1	艦	1	鑑	6	丸	2	緩	1	器	2	希	1	求	1	去	1	寄	1	擬	1		
韓	2	伎	1	危	1	机	1	岸	2	棄	2	鬼	1	漁	1	凶	1	疑	6	九	16		
企	1	幾	1	既	1	記	2	飢	1	犠	2	義	2	競	2	恐	1	拠	2	泣	2		
紀	1	菊	1	揮	1	期	1	貴	1	却	1	客	1	斤	1	謹	1	鏡	9	巨	9		
喜	1	弓	1	吉	2	宜	1	欺	2	嗅	1	朽	1	緊	1	錦	1	巾	1	共	1		
議	1	糾	1	丘	1	喫	1	却	1	窮	1	嗅	1			均	1	恭	1				
及	1	拠	13	宮	2	旧	2	吸	1	急	1	魚	1			襟	1	近	1				
拒	1	強	1	挙	2	救	2	給	2	凶	1	峡	1					吟	1				
狂	1	業	2	享	2	虚	1	況	1	僅	1	玉	1										
叫	1	勤	2	教	2	境	2	橋	16			禁	1										
暁	2			琴	2	凝	2	筋	2														
菌	2																						

Table A.2: The topmost decomposition operations for the regular-use Chinese characters in Japanese – Part II.

C	O	C	O	C	O	C	O	C	O	C	O	C	O	C	O	C	O	C	O	C	O	C	O	C	O
区	8	句	5	苦	2	駆	1	具	2	惧	1	愚	2	空	2	勲	2	偶	1	遇	4	隅	4	串	16
屈	6	掘	1	窟	2	熊	2	繰	1	君	6	訓	1	型	1	薫	1	軍	2	郡	2	群	1
兄	2	刑	1	形	1	系	2	径	2	茎	2	係	1	傾	1	契	2	計	1	恵	1	啓	2
掲	1	渓	0	憩	1	蛍	2	敬	2	景	2	軽	4	鯨	1	携	1	継	0	詣	6	慶	1
憬	1	稽	6	穴	2	血	2	鶏	1	芸	2	迎	1	潔	4	隙	0	劇	2	件	1	激	0
桁	2	欠	2	建	0	研	0	決	1	結	1	傑	1	剣	1	月	2	犬	1	健	1	見	1
券	1	肩	1	検	1	嫌	1	県	1	倹	1	兼	1	権	0	拳	1	軒	1	謙	3	険	2
圏	3	堅	1	験	1	懸	1	献	4	絹	1	遣	1	言	2	憲	1	賢	2	原	1	鍵	1
繭	2	顕	5	源	1	個	2	元	1	幻	0	玄	1	誇	15	股	2	限	3	虎	6	孤	1
弧	1	減	2	枯	1	後	6	己	2	戸	1	古	2	語	1	鼓	1	股	1	口	1	五	0
互	15	故	6	呉	1	功	1	庫	0	湖	1	悟	0	荒	1	誤	2	鋼	2	后	2	工	15
公	2	午	1	孔	1	坑	1	娯	6	広	6	碁	6	郊	1	効	1	護	1	拘	1	好	1
江	1	勾	1	行	1	洪	1	巧	1	抗	1	甲	1	黄	1	香	0	向	7	校	14	肯	2
侯	1	考	2	恒	0	高	1	孝	1	控	1	攻	1	稿	2	喉	9	幸	1	港	2	耕	1
航	1	厚	1	降	1	鉱	1	皇	0	綱	1	梗	1	込	1	頃	1	候	14	谷	16	硬	1
絞	1	貢	1	溝	1	合	1	構	1	剛	0	傲	0	墾	6	懇	1	告	2	佐	1	講	0
購	3	項	1	号	1	酷	1	拷	14	骨	1	駒	1	座	1	才	1	今	16	災	1	刻	3
国	1	乞	0	穀	1	差	5	獄	6	鎖	1	座	1	済	1	斎	1	左	1	菜	2	昆	1
恨	1	黒	1	婚	1	栽	1	痕	1	採	1	済	6	際	1	在	0	再	1	剤	1	沙	2
査	2	根	1	唆	1	塞	1	詐	5	察	1	際	0	埼	1	酢	2	細	2	錯	1	妻	1
采	5	砂	1	宰	1	削	1	歳	1	柵	1	索	1	祭	1	擦	1	材	1	皿	1	最	1
罪	7	砕	1	催	1	利	1	昨	1	殺	1	傘	0	撮	1	史	1	搾	1	賛	1	財	1
冊	0	債	2	桟	1	蚕	1	拶	1	産	1	氏	1	散	1	使	1	雑	1	始	1	咲	2
山	0	崎	7	土	6	子	1	惨	1	止	1	志	1	仕	1	恣	1	酸	1	摯	1	三	1
斬	0	札	0	死	1	糸	1	至	0	伺	1	私	1	飼	1	誌	1	司	1	識	1	残	1
矢	1	参	1	肢	0	嗣	1	思	1	施	1	資	1	似	1	鹿	1	刺	1	実	1	市	1
枝	2	暫	1	歯	1	寺	0	試	1	詩	0	餌	1	璽	6	漆	1	雌	16	寂	1	視	2
紫	1	旨	2	滋	0	慈	1	次	1	磁	1	璽	6	鹿	1	斜	1	事	5	舟		賜	1
諮	1	祉	1	失	1	室	6	辞	1	耳	1	湿	1	赦	1	州		式	1			治	1
持	1	詞	1	車	6	舎	1	磁	6	自	0	捨	0	爵	1			質	1			軸	2
七	16	示	16	勺	0	尺	0	射	1	餌	1	施	1	酒	1			煮	1			芝	1
写	2	時	2	朱	15	取	15	首	1	璽	1	詩	1	囚				弱	1			謝	0
邪	1	叱	1	呪	1	授	1	儒		湿	1	耳	0					腫	1			手	4
主	6	社	2							捨	0	儒						州				趣	2
寿		守	6							釈	1											秀	
		受								樹													

Table A.3: The topmost decomposition operations for the regular-use Chinese characters in Japanese – Part III.

C	O	C	O	C	O	C	O	C	O	C	O	C	O	C	O	C	O	C	O	C	O	C	O
周	7	宗	2	拾	1	秋	1	臭	2	修	1	袖	1	終	1	羞	6	習	2	週	4	就	1
衆	2	集	2	渋	2	酬	1	醜	1	蹴	2	襲	2	十	0	汁	1	充	2	住	1	柔	2
塾	2	従	2	出	9	銃	4	獣	1	縦	1	叔	2	祝	1	宿	2	淑	5	粛	16	縮	6
殉	2	熟	2	循	1	述	1	術	14	俊	1	春	1	瞬	1	旬	2	巡	1	盾	2	准	0
升	2	純	2	緒	1	順	1	準	2	潤	1	遵	1	処	4	初	1	所	7	書	16	庶	1
沼	1	少	1	召	2	諸	1	女	0	如	1	助	1	序	6	叙	2	徐	1	除	2	小	1
章	1	昭	2	宵	1	匠	8	床	6	抄	1	肖	1	尚	2	招	14	承	0	商	14	松	1
象	1	紹	2	奨	2	将	1	詳	1	症	6	祥	1	称	1	笑	1	唱	1	詔	1	渉	1
場	1	傷	1	蒸	16	勝	1	条	2	晶	2	焼	1	焦	1	硝	1	粧	1	償	1	証	1
植	1	上	1	飾	2	冗	0	壊	1	彰	1	障	1	憧	1	衝	1	色	6	常	1	礁	1
臣	0	畳	2	身	0	縄	1	嘱	1	状	1	乗	6	城	1	浄	2	心	0	拭	1	情	1
真	2	芯	1	深	1	触	1	侵	1	嬢	1	錠	2	譲	1	醸	15	娠	1	申	14	伸	2
薪	3	針	1	人	16	紳	16	進	4	信	1	津	1	辱	1	尻	2	新	1	振	1	浸	1
図	1	親	1	吹	0	刃	2	炊	1	森	2	診	1	神	1	唇	6	尋	6	審	1	震	1
穂	3	水	1	随	2	垂	1	枢	1	成	6	迅	1	寝	2	慎	2	酔	2	腎	14	須	1
是	1	錘	2	政	0	髄	0	性	1	省	1	粋	1	甚	1	陣	1	裾	1	遂	1	睡	1
勢	2	井	2	誠	1	正	1	製	1	誓	1	西	1	袁	0	推	1	姓	1	寸	1	性	2
斥	0	斉	1	赤	1	星	1	析	1	席	1	凄	1	拠	1	制	1	盛	2	征	1	晴	1
説	16	石	1	籍	0	昔	0	川	1	拙	1	静	1	請	1	清	1	醒	1	婿	1	夕	1
洗	1	績	1	扇	2	切	1	旋	1	仙	1	窃	1	隻	1	惜	1	戚	1	税	1	跡	1
箋	1	舌	1	銃	1	千	1	膳	1	船	1	占	2	煎	2	設	1	専	1	摂	2	浅	2
善	1	染	2	疎	6	栓	2	塑	1	遷	1	戦	1	薦	1	宜	1	腺	1	泉	1	措	1
粗	1	銭	1	荘	1	潜	1	送	1	繞	1	狙	1	阻	1	羨	1	鮮	2	争	1	走	1
奏	2	組	2	窓	1	漸	1	喪	15	遡	1	礎	1	挿	4	桑	2	早	1	掃	2	曹	1
遭	4	相	2	耐	1	訴	1	燥	1	倉	1	捜	1	装	2	僧	1	巣	1	層	1	憎	2
蔵	2	爽	2	隊	4	草	1	束	1	霜	1	痩	1	藻	1	造	1	想	1	速	6	側	2
測	1	槽	1	沢	1	創	1	賊	1	続	2	促	1	則	1	息	2	像	1	孫	1	尊	2
損	1	贈	2			操	6	汰	15	打	15	卒	1	唾	1	存	6	捉	2	袋	2	太	4
対	1	遜	1			即	1	怠	1	胎	1	妥	1	帯	5	堕	1	惰	1	題	4	逮	1
替	1	体	1			属	1	態	1	託	1	大	4	代	1	泰	1	堆	2	達	4	滝	1
宅	2	貸	2			多	1	拓	2			濯	1	諾	1	台	1	第	2			脱	1
						待	1									濁	1	但	1				
						卓	2																

Table A.4: The topmost decomposition operations for the regular-use Chinese characters in Japanese – Part IV.

C	O	C	O	C	O	C	O	C	O	C	O	C	O	C	O	C	O	C	O	C	O	C	O	C	O
奪	2	棚	1	誰	1	誕	16	丹	16	旦	2	担	1	単	2	炭	2	胆	2	探	1	淡	1	短	1
嘆	1	端	1	綻	1	知	1	鍛	1	抽	1	秩	13	男	2	段	2	断	2	弾	1	暖	16	談	1
壇	1	地	2	池	4	蓄	1	値	2	庁	1	注	1	致	1	遅	1	痴	1	稚	1	置	1	緻	1
竹	0	畜	1	逐	2	忠	2	築	6	兆	2	直	1	窒	1	茶	1	着	6	嫡	15	中	1	仲	1
虫	0	沖	2	宙	2	弔	2	朝	1	脹	1	渡	1	昼	1	柱	1	衷	1	酎	1	鋳	1	駐	1
著	1	貯	1	丁	1	鳥	0	懲	1	通	2	党	2	町	1	長	1	腸	1	帳	1	張	1	彫	1
眺	1	釣	1	頂	6	聴	16	墜	1	底	1	南	2	貼	1	超	6	沈	1	珍	1	徴	1	嘲	1
潮	1	澄	6	調	4	椎	1	定	2	提	1	悩	1	勅	1	捗	1	漬	1	坪	1	朕	1	陳	2
賃	1	鎮	2	追	4	弟	1	堤	1	溺	1	迫	1	痛	1	塚	1	亭	1	徹	1	帝	1	鶴	0
低	6	呈	2	廷	1	偵	4	敵	4	投	2	盤	1	程	2	邸	1	締	15	殿	1	撤	1	訂	6
庭	2	遷	4	停	1	適	6	都	6	筒	4			豆	2	哲	1	伝	1	倒	1	電	1	的	1
笛	2	摘	6	滴	1	展	4	当	4	得	6			悼	1	田	1	土	0	搭	4	努	1	天	1
典	1	店	1	点	1	途	1	透	1	豚	2			統	1	賭	1	到	1	毒	1	搭	1	斗	5
怒	2	妬	0	徒	1	灯	1	洞	2	尿	1			頓	2	東	1	陶	1	篤	1	独	2	度	1
唐	6	刀	5	冬	1	討	1	特	1	婆	2			任	2	盗	1	踏	1	二	1	丼	1	凍	1
湯	1	痘	7	桃	5	答	2	屯	7	売	1			納	1	稲	1	童	1	忍	1	寧	8	棟	1
藤	2	瞳	2	登	6	同	7	鍋	1	肌	0			罵	1	堂	1	鈍	1	博	1	濃	1	謄	2
栃	1	凸	1	騰	7	匿	8	乳	6	犯	1			剝	1	徳	1	二	2	発	2	麦	1	銅	1
奈	2	内	1	峠	1	謎	6	燃	0	販	1			八	2	貪	1	伴	1	培	1	頌	1	読	1
肉	0	虹	1	突	2	入	1	廃	1	疲	1			比	1	難	1	妃	1	悲	1	否	1	那	5
年	16	念	0	梨	6	粘	0	拍	6	備	1			秘	1	能	1	悲	2	膝	1	扉	1	匂	1
波	1	派	1	日	1	覇	1	馬	2	服	1			微	1	拝	1	膝	1	評	1	負	1	熱	1
配	1	排	7	捻	0	届	2	輩	1					俵	1	梅	1	評	2	頻	1	毎	1	把	1
賠	1	白	1	破	1	箸	6	泊	0					貧	1	舶	1	頻	1	訃	1	腹	1	買	16
縛	1	爆	1	敗	0	半	2	畑	2					怖	1	皮	1	訃	0	賦	1			漠	1
罰	1	閥	4	反	1	畔	1	氾	2					敷	1	被	1	賦	1	復	1			阪	1
板	1	版	2	班	6	番	2	般	2					副	1	鼻	1	復	1					範	2
繁	2	藩	6	晩	1	眉	2	蛮	2							賓	1							彼	2
披	1	肥	0	非	1	百	2	美	2							阜	1							碑	4
罷	1	避	1	尾	1	猫	2	氷	2							膚	1							必	5
泌	1	筆	2	姫	1	布	0	扶	0							幅	1							赴	1
秒	16	病	1	描	0	富	1	普	1															武	1
夫	1	父	1	付	1	風	2	伏	1															複	1
浮	1	婦	1	符	2																				
部	1			封	0																				

Table A.5: The topmost decomposition operations for the regular-use Chinese characters in Japanese – Part V.

C	O	C	O	C	O	C	O	C	O	C	O	C	O	C	O	C	O	C	O	C	O	C	O
覆	2	払	1	沸	1	仏	1	物	1	粉	2	紛	1	雲	2	噴	1	墳	1	慎	1	奮	2
分	2	文	0	聞	7	内	2	平	15	兵	2	併	2	並	6	柄	1	陛	1	閉	7	塀	1
幣	2	弊	2	蔽	2	餅	1	米	0	壁	2	璧	2	癖	4	別	1	蔑	1	片	0	辺	4
返	4	変	2	偏	0	遍	4	編	1	弁	2	便	1	薄	2	歩	2	保	2	哺	1	捕	1
補	1	宝	1	母	1	募	2	墓	2	慕	2	暮	1	俸	1	傲	1	包	0	芳	1	崩	2
奉	2	報	1	抱	1	放	1	法	2	泡	2	胞	15	亡	2	乏	1	峰	1	砲	2	妨	1
訪	2	防	6	蜂	6	豊	1	飽	1	褒	15	剖	2	紡	2	凡	7	牧	1	坊	5	僕	6
忘	2	貌	2	房	2	膨	6	某	1	冒	2	北	16	木	0	膜	1	枕	1	帽	2	摩	16
墨	6	撲	1	暴	1	勃	2	謀	1	頬	2	奔	1	翻	1	岬	1	密	1	睦	7	末	1
抹	1	魔	1	没	1	妹	1	堀	2	本	16	埋	1	幕	2	娘	0	名	1	麻	0	脈	1
妙	1	万	6	毎	1	慢	1	枚	1	昧	1	夢	1	魅	6	綿	1	麺	1	又	1	明	1
迷	4	民	1	満	1	矛	1	漫	1	未	16	免	1	面	1	門	6	躍	1	蜜	1	匁	16
毛	0	冥	2	眠	1	銘	1	務	1	無	1	目	0	黙	1	薬	1	勇	1	命	2	由	2
冶	1	妄	1	盟	1	弥	1	鳴	1	網	1	約	1	訳	6	融	1	容	1	茂	5	悠	2
油	1	喩	1	盲	1	論	1	猛	1	役	1	唯	1	友	2	要	1	養	1	問	7	予	1
郵	1	誉	1	野	1	裕	1	遊	1	癒	1	味	1	憂	1	窯	1	濫	1	闇	11	揚	2
余	1	葉	1	愉	1	幼	1	用	1	雄	1	妖	1	洋	1	裸	1	陸	1	与	1	謡	15
揺	1	抑	1	猶	1	溶	1	腰	1	様	1	瘍	1	踊	1	陸	1	旅	1	庸	6	雷	1
頼	1	絡	1	預	1	酪	1	欲	1	翌	1	卵	6	拉	1	侶	1	臨	1	擁	1	吏	6
利	1	里	1	陽	0	痢	1	辣	1	乱	1	翼	1	覧	1	僚	1	鈴	2	来	1	慄	1
略	1	柳	1	沃	1	料	1	竜	1	粒	1	璃	1	量	1	例	1	弄	2	欄	1	慮	6
了	1	両	1	落	1	緑	1	涼	1	猟	1	陵	1	輪	6	隣	2	和	1	律	1	療	2
瞭	1	糧	1	理	1	令	1	林	1	列	1	倫	1	戻	2	裂	1			寮	1	霊	2
累	1	齢	6	流	1	暦	1	礼	1	路	1	劣	1	烈	0	労	6			連	2	廉	6
隷	1	錬	2	良	1	炉	1	歴	1	六	1	録	1	露	2	論	2			郎	1	朗	1
練	1	廊	1	麗	6	楼	6	賂	1											話	1	賄	1
浪	1	惑	2	呂	2	枠	2	籠	1														
脇	1							腕	1														

Acknowledgments

First and foremost, the author sincerely thanks Professor Keiichi KANEKO (Tokyo University of Agriculture and Technology, Koganei, Tokyo, Japan) for his insightful advice and comments regarding Chinese characters and related subjects. And, from the same institution, Professors Tomoko HONGO and Takao TOMONO have been of valuable help when collecting information for Section 5.6.2.

The author is also grateful to Professor Takeyuki NAGAO (Shizuoka Institute of Science and Technology, Fukuroi, Shizuoka, Japan) for sharing his views and experience with respect to natural languages and writing systems in general, and to Professor Sanggyu SHIN (Advanced Institute of Industrial Technology, Shinagawa, Tokyo, Japan) for his advice on Korean.

Several characters in this book were rendered using the "Tangut Yinchuan" font by Jing Yongshi, the "Mojikyo" font

234   *Acknowledgments*

(今昔文字鏡) by the Mojikyo Institute and courtesy of AI-NET
Corporation, and the "Ancient Chinese characters project" by
Wikimedia Commons (public domain). The world map is from
Wikimedia Commons (public domain).

Finally, the author thanks the Vietnamese Nôm Preservation
Foundation for their permission to include in this book materials
from their digital library.

本書の出版は神奈川大学出版会の助成による

(The publication of this book was supported by
Kanagawa University Press.)

Index

algebra 104
algorithm 132
associativity 126
ateji 57

bronze 11

chain 176
Chữ nôm 23
class 146
combination 47
compound 30, 46
connectivity 128

decomposition 104
derivative cognate 48
distance

mathematical 170
morpho-semantic 162
dōkun-iji 95

encoding 157

form 74

geography 13
graph 66
gukja 28
gyōninben 200

hanja 22
history 10

ideogram 45

236　*Index*

instance 146, 150

kanji 14
key 60
kokuji 24

loanword 57
local 24
logogram 59

modality 182
model 146

ninben 182

object 146, 150
ontology 145
operation 114
oracle bone 11

path 71
phonetic loan 47
phono-semantic 46
pictogram 45
pronunciation 51

radical 48, 60
rationale 3

reading 53
　　kun 54
　　on 54
relation 67
　　morpho-semantic 83
　　morphological 68
　　phonetic 87, 94
　　semantic 73
ryakuji 33

seal 12
set
　　radical 109
　　real 107
　　support 110
simplification 14, 208
six writings 44
stroke 39
style 80

transcription 58

variant 73

writing order 41
writing system 17

yakja 33

Antoine BOSSARD is an Associate Professor at the Graduate School of Science, Kanagawa University, Japan. He received his B.E. and M.E. degrees from Université de Caen Basse-Normandie, France, in 2005 and 2007, respectively, and his Ph.D. degree from Tokyo University of Agriculture and Technology, Japan, in 2011. His research is focused on two main topics: graph theory, with applications to interconnection networks (addressing issues such as routing and fault tolerance); and natural languages, especially writing systems. He is the author of multiple peer-reviewed publications in these fields. He also authored the textbook "A Gentle Introduction to Functional Programming in English" (Ohmsha, 2017), which was written for students of his functional programming lecture.

Antoine BOSSARD（ボサール・アントワーヌ）神奈川大学理学部情報科学科准教授
　フランス生まれ。2007 年、(仏) 国立カン大学大学院理学研究科数理情報学専攻博士前期課程修了。2007 年、来日。2011 年、東京農工大学大学院工学府電子情報工学専攻博士後期課程修了。2011 年、東京農工大学大学院生物システム応用科学府特任助教。2012 年、産業技術大学院大学情報アーキテクチャ専攻助教。2015 年、神奈川大学理学部情報科学科助教、2017 年から現職。専門分野は主にグラフ理論、特に相互結合網と経路選択問題、および自然言語。この分野で論文多数を執筆。著書に、担当科目「関数プログラミング」の学生向けの教科書『関数プログラミング入門, in English!』（2017 年、オーム社）がある。

Chinese Characters, Deciphered

2018 年 3 月 10 日初版発行

著　作　者　Antoine BOSSARD

発　行　所　神奈川大学出版会
〒 221-8686
神奈川県横浜市神奈川区六角橋 3-27-1
電話（045）481-5661

発　売　所　丸善出版株式会社
〒 101-0051
東京都千代田区神田神保町 2-17
電話（03）3512-3256
http://pub.maruzen.co.jp/

編集・制作協力　丸善雄松堂株式会社

©Antoine BOSSARD, 2018　　　　　　　　　Printed in Japan

印刷・製本／三美印刷株式会社
ISBN978-4-906279-14-2 C3004